Behold and See 6

Workbook

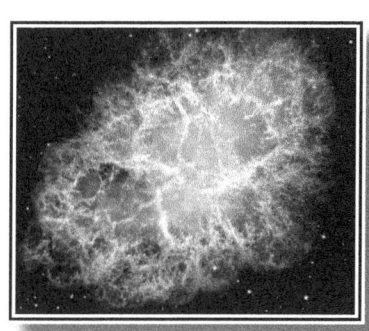

Catholic Heritage Curricula

1-800-490-7713   www.chcweb.com

Experiments: Although every effort has been made to ensure the safety of the experiments within this workbook, parents are responsible for taking appropriate safety measures and supervising students during experiments. Catholic Heritage Curricula disclaims all responsibility for any injury or risk which is incurred as a result of the use of any of the material suggested for experiments.

Web Links: Parental supervision is strongly advised when your child is visiting recommended website links. At the time of this printing these links contained helpful information that was age-appropriate. Be advised that good links can change frequently, becoming inappropriate or no longer available. Because of this, please visit recommended web links beforehand and supervise student during his online visit as he explores the activity, video, or experiment.

Credits:

Diagrams and illustrations: AnneMarie Johnson

Image Credits: cover: © Johannes Kroemer/Tetra Images/Corbis; cover: © iStockphoto / Thinkstock; cover: © Hemera / Thinkstock; cover: NASA, ESA, J. Hester, A. Loll (ASU); cover: © Jupiterimages / Thinkstock; pg. i: © iStockphoto / Thinkstock; pg. i: © Hemera / Thinkstock; pg. i: NASA, ESA, J. Hester, A. Loll (ASU); pg. i: © Jupiterimages / Thinkstock; pg. iii: © iStockphoto / Thinkstock; pg. iii: © iStockphoto / Thinkstock; pg. iii: © iStockphoto / Thinkstock; pg. iii: © iStockphoto / Thinkstock; pg. iii: © iStockphoto / Thinkstock; pg. 4: (x17) Hemera / Thinkstock; pg. 4: © Pasieka / Photo Researchers, Inc.; pg. 6: © iStockphoto / Thinkstock; pg. 82: © Ingrid Prats / Shutterstock.com; pg. 82: © Dr Ajay Kumar Singh / Shutterstock.com; pg. 82: © Dr Ajay Kumar Singh / Shutterstock.com; back cover: © oksana.perkins / Shutterstock.com; back cover: © ephotographer/Shutterstock; back cover: © oorka / Shutterstock.com; back cover: © Poznukhov Yuriy / Shutterstock.com; back cover: © markrhiggins / Shutterstock.com; back cover: © Valerie Potapova / Shutterstock.com

ISBN: 978-0-9851642-2-5

© 2012 Catholic Heritage Curricula   2019 Edition

This book is under copyright. All rights reserved. No part of this book may be reproduced in any form by any means—electronic, mechanical, or graphic—without prior written permission. Thank you for honoring copyright law.

For more information:
Catholic Heritage Curricula
1-800-490-7713
www.chcweb.com

Printed by Integrated Books International
Dulles, Virginia
June 2020

TABLE OF CONTENTS

Chapter Questions

    Unit 1 Workbook Questions, *1*

    Unit 2 Workbook Questions, *41*

    Unit 3 Workbook Questions, *74*

Unit Tests

    Unit 1 Test, *38*

    Unit 2 Test, *70*

    Unit 3 Test, *114*

Answer Key

    Unit 1 Answer Key, *143*

    Unit 2 Answer Key, *147*

    Unit 3 Answer Key, *150*

Star-Gazing Activities

    Star-Gazing Activities, *73*

    Star-Gazing Test, *78*

Experiments

    Supply List, *117*

    Unit 1 Experiments #1-20, *119*

    Unit 2 Experiments #21-25, *137*

    Unit 3 Experiment #26, *142*

For a detailed, daily lesson plan, see *Behold and See 6 Daily Lesson Plans* at *www.chcweb.com*.

This accompanying student workbook to *Behold and See 6* provides student-friendly exercises, research assignments, extension activities, experiments, and tests. The "Check It Out!" web links listed throughout the workbook may be explored as time allows. Interactive links, extension activities, and video clips can make difficult concepts easier to grasp.

Chapter questions and tests within these pages provide clear objectives for learning and review. Encourage your student to refer to the text to complete the workbook pages and Chapter Reviews. The Unit Tests are designed to be given "closed-book." The Answer Key (beginning on page 143) may be removed at the parent's discretion.

UNIT 1   Chapter 2

Word Scramble

Unscramble these words, taken from the new words learned in this chapter.

1. SAMS   _ _ _ _

2. MUVLEO   _ _ _ _ _ _

3. YTESDIN   _ _ _ _ _ _ _

4. CNCISEE   _ _ _ _ _ _ _

Fill in the Blank

Now use the unscrambled words, above, to fill in the right answers, below!

1. how much space an object takes up ....

2. a systematic way of exploring the world God created ....

3. the amount of matter that is in an object ....

4. the measurement of how much matter is packed into a certain space
....

Science Notebook

Write out the six steps of the Scientific Method in your Science Notebook.

Density and the Buoyant Force

Answer the questions and fill in the blanks.

1. An apple floats in water. Is it more or less dense than water?
   ....

2. Is there more matter in a cubic inch of apple or in a cubic inch of water?
   ....

3. An unidentified object is thrown into the swimming pool. If it is denser than water it will .... If it is less dense than water it will ....

4. When Mike's mom makes doughnuts, she deep-fries them in hot oil. When she first places the circle of dough into the pot of oil, the dough sinks to the bottom. This means that uncooked doughnuts are .... dense than hot oil. As the doughnuts cook, the baking powder produces bubbles of carbon dioxide, which make the doughnuts expand. Eventually, the doughnuts fill with so much carbon dioxide that they rise to the top of the pot of oil. The doughnuts are now .... dense than the hot oil.

5. Nick holds an object underwater. He has to lift it up to keep it in position, because it is .... dense than water. Christie also holds an object underwater. Her object is less dense than water, so she has to *[lift it up / push it down]* to keep it in position.

Science Notebook

Write out the definitions of mass, volume, density, gravity, and the buoyant force in your Science Notebook.

What Is True?

Mark "T" if the statement is true; mark "F" if the statement is false.

1. .... The more matter there is in an object, the greater the force of gravity will be on the object.

2. .... The upward "push" which water gives to objects is called the buoyant force.

3. .... Gravity is a force that acts on empty space.

4. .... Density is the measurement of how much matter is packed into a certain space.

5. .... The buoyant force makes you feel heavier when you are underwater.

6. .... When an object is less dense than water, the buoyant force makes it sink.

7. .... Objects sink when they are denser than the water they displace.

CHECK IT OUT!

Density of different liquids: https://www.exploratorium.edu/science_explorer/glitter.html
Condiment diver: https://www.exploratorium.edu/snacks/condiment_diver/index.html
Video for each element: http://www.periodicvideos.com/

Chapter 2

Element, Compound, or Mixture?

Label the following pictures and sentences as elements, compounds, or mixtures.

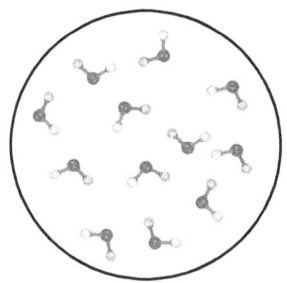 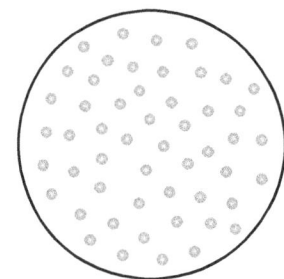 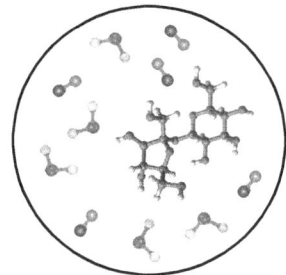

1. .... 2. .... 3. ....

4. Carbon dioxide is made out of carbon dioxide molecules, each of which is made of one carbon atom and two oxygen atoms. Carbon dioxide is a/an ....

5. A certain substance is made only of carbon atoms, so it is a/an ....

6. Chlorine is made of chlorine atoms. Chlorine is a/an ....

7. Salt is made of salt molecules. Salt is a/an ....

Science Notebook

Draw the element, compound, and mixture diagrams (above) in your Science Notebook. If desired, you may color the diagrams as shown in the textbook, Figure 2.7.

Classifying Matter

Use the chart below to fill in the blanks. Then draw the chart in your Science Notebook.

1. The two types of matter are .... and ....

2. The two types of pure substances are .... and ....

3. A mixture can be separated into its parts by using .... processes.

4. A compound can be separated into its parts by using .... processes.

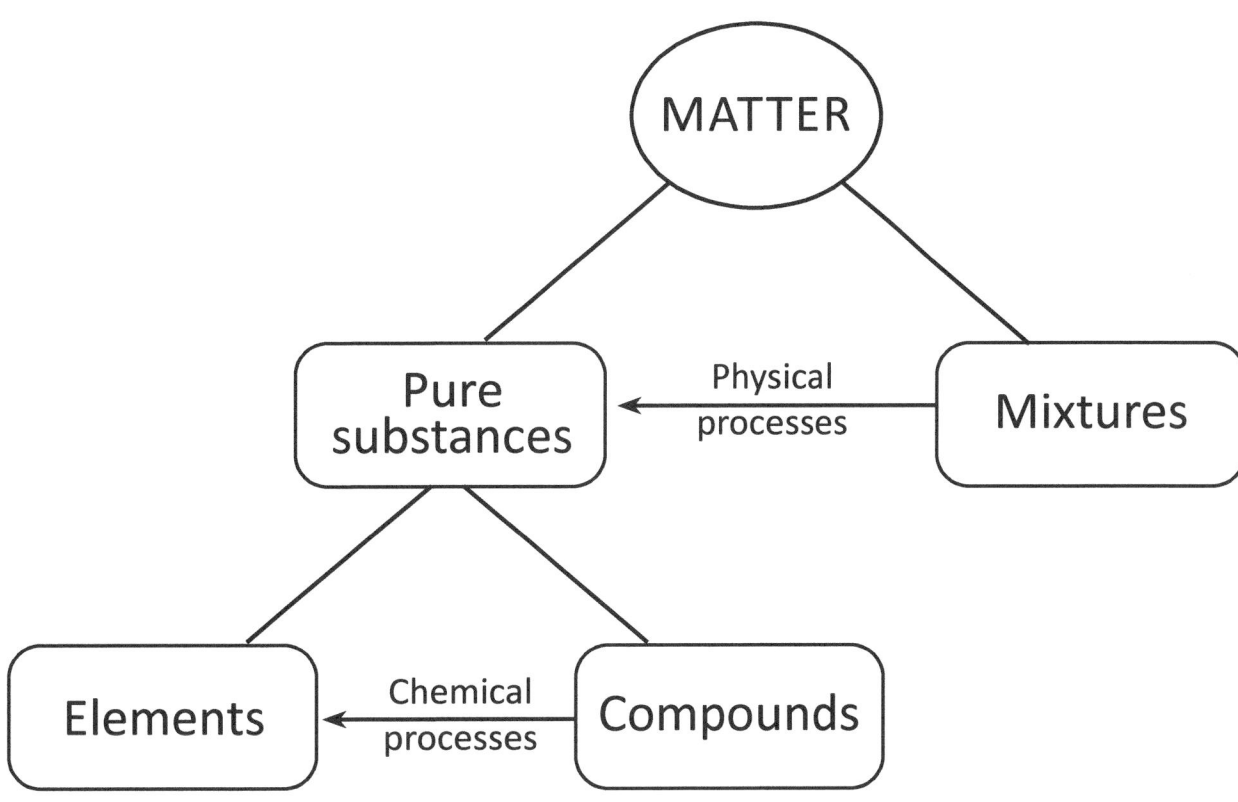

Atoms

Fill in the blanks to complete the sentences.

1. The inside of an atom is mostly ....

2. The center, or nucleus, of an atom is made of tiny particles called .... and ....

3. If we break apart an atom of gold, we are left with ...., ..., and ....

Label the Parts of an Atom

Label the parts of an atom. Next, draw it in your Science Notebook and label its parts.

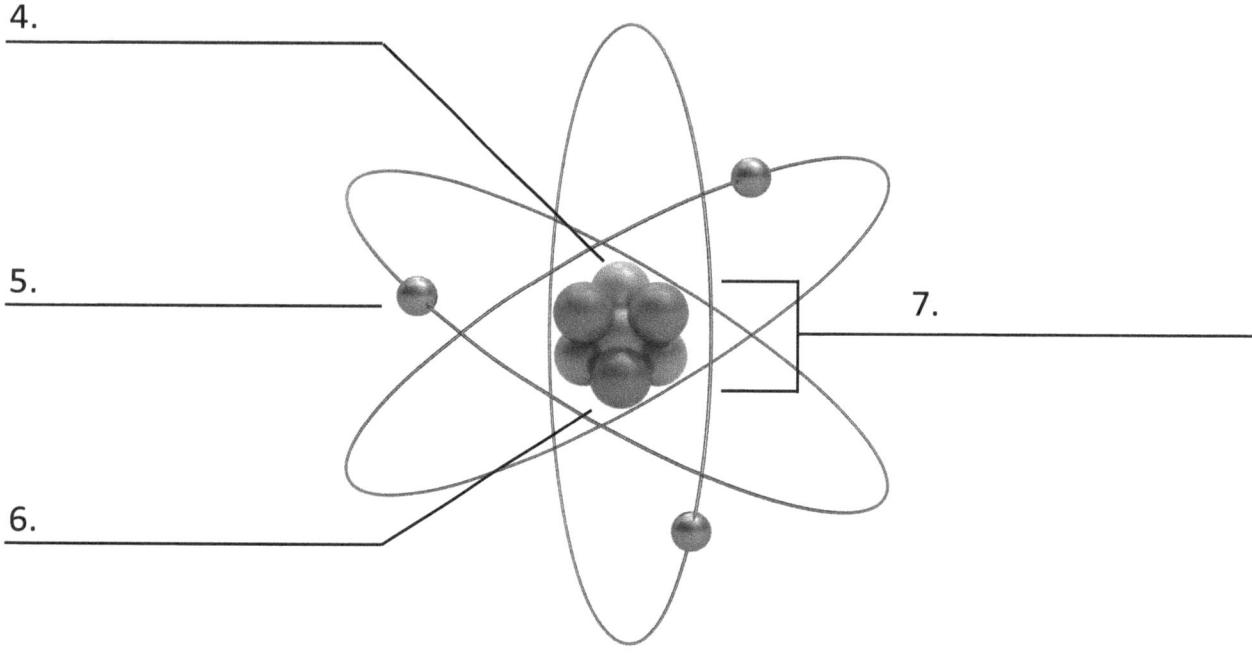

4. _____

5. _____

6. _____

7. _____

Chapter 2 Review

Answer in complete sentences.

1. Can the volume of an object change even if its mass does not?

   ....

2. List the six steps of the Scientific Method in order.

   ....

   ....

   ....

   ....

   ....

   ....

3. What is density?

   ....

   ....

4. What is the buoyant force?

   ....

   ....

5. What is an atom?

   ....

   ....

6. What is an element?

   ....

   ....

7. What is a compound?
   ....
   ....

8. What are molecules?
   ....
   ....

9. What is a mixture?
   ....
   ....

10. What is a pure substance?
    ....
    ....

11. What is the nucleus of an atom?
    ....
    ....

12. What are electrons?
    ....
    ....

Chapter 3

Liquid, Solid, or Gas?

Fill in the blanks to complete the sentences.

1. Matter changes from one state to another because of a change in ....

2. The energy that makes atoms and molecules move and jiggle is called heat energy, or .... energy.

3. Atoms are spaced farthest apart in this state of matter: ....

4. A substance changes from a liquid to a solid through a process called ....

5. A substance changes from a solid to a liquid through a process called ....

6. A substance changes from a gas to a liquid through a process called ....

7. At 25°F, water is a ....

8. At 3000°F, iron is a ....

9. At -400°F, oxygen is a ....

10. At 200°F, rubbing alcohol is a ....

11. At 50°F, mercury is a ....

Fill in the Blanks: Solid, Gas, and Liquid

Use the word bank below to label each change of state in the diagram.

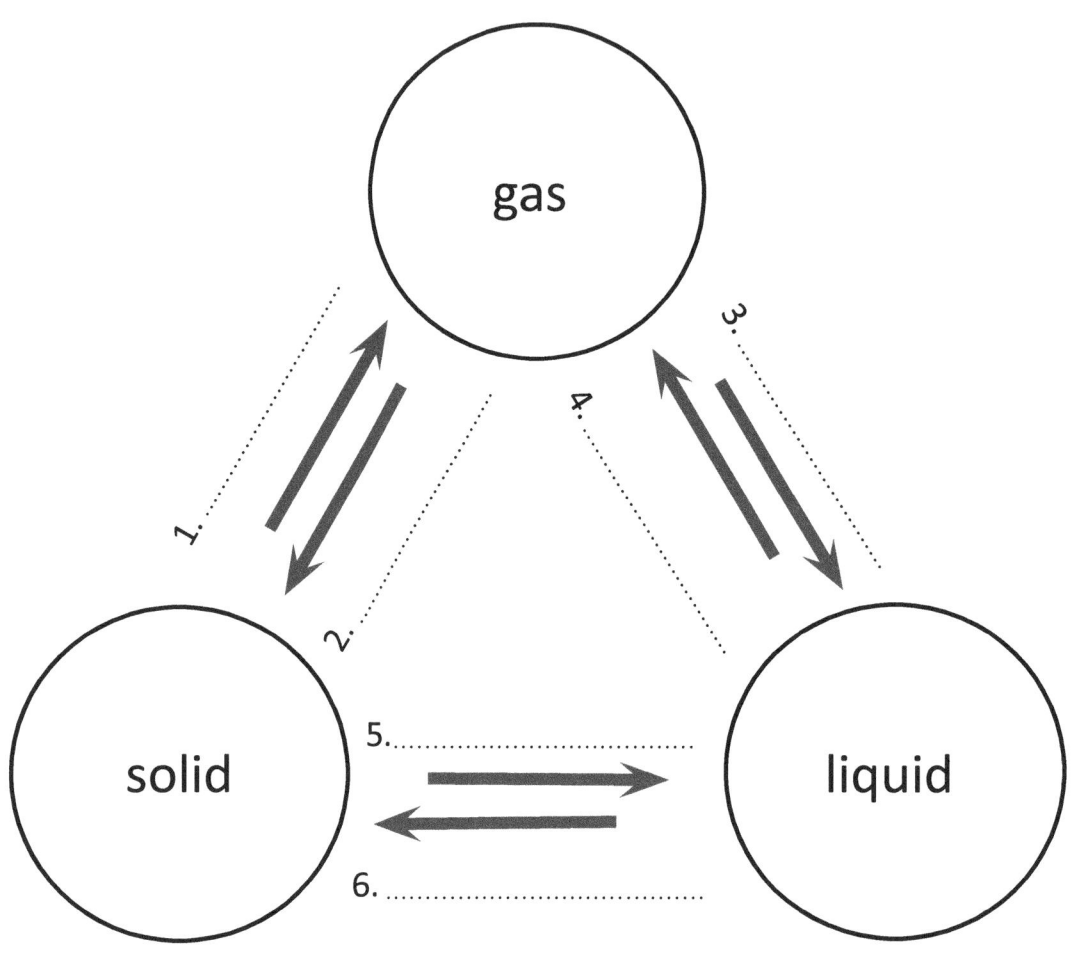

| freezing | condensation | sublimation |
| vaporization | melting | deposition |

Science Notebook

Draw and label the above chart in your Science Notebook.

Solubility

Fill in the blanks to complete the sentences.

1. Mixtures that are made when one material dissolves into another are called ....

2. .... is the scientific name for the "dissolver," that is, the gas, liquid, or solid in which another material is dissolved.

3. When a material is able to be dissolved, we say that it is ....

4. Some materials are .... in water. This means they will not dissolve in water.

5. When no more sugar will dissolve in water, we say the water is ....

6. Water is called the .... because it is so good at dissolving things.

CHECK IT OUT!

Liquid nitrogen: https://education.jlab.org/frost/
Non-Newtonian fluids: https://www.exploratorium.edu/science_explorer/ooze.html
Solutions and crystals: https://www.exploratorium.edu/cooking/seasoning/kitchen/activity-saltsculpture.html
Science of cooking: https://www.exploratorium.edu/cooking

Chapter 3 Review

Answer in complete sentences.

1. What makes matter change from one state to another?

   ....

   ....

2. When an object is heated, do its atoms and molecules become more or less energetic?

   ....

3. What is evaporation?

   ....

   ....

   ....

4. What is condensation?

   ....

   ....

   ....

5. At what temperature does water freeze?

   ....

6. At what temperature does water boil?

   ....

7. *Fill in the blanks:* An object .... when it is heated and .... when it is cooled.

8. Why does water expand when it is frozen?

   ....

   ....

   ....

9. What is solubility?

   ....

   ....

10. *Match the pictures at left to their correct definitions at right.*

    i. ....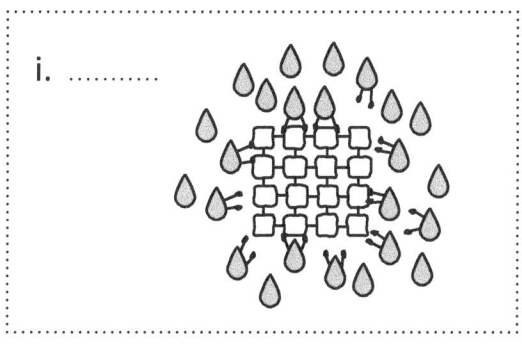

    a. A sugar crystal being "pulled" apart by water molecules

    ii. ....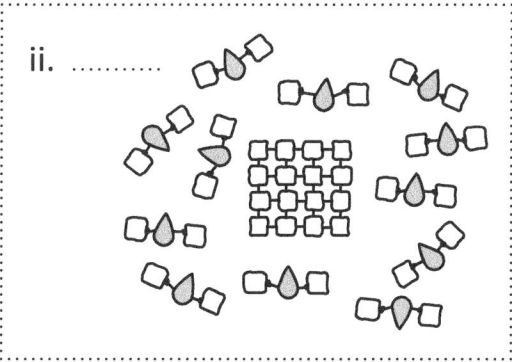

    b. A sugar crystal as it first enters the water

    iii. ....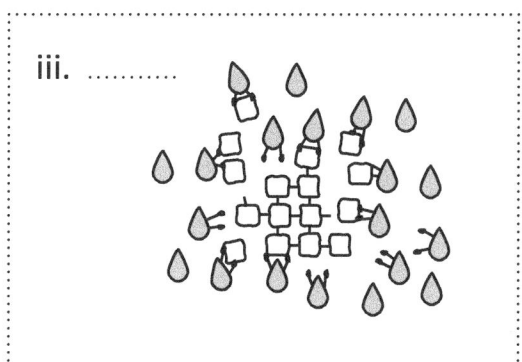

    c. A sugar crystal in a saturated solution of water and sugar

Chapter 3

Chapter 4

Word Scramble

Unscramble these words, all of which are examples of "work."

1. pwese   _ (_) _ _ _

2. ptchoscoh   _ _ _ _ _ (_) _ _

3. uirsnbgh   _ (_) _ _ _ _ _

4. lwka   _ _ _ (_)

5. hiisnfg   (_) _ _ _ _ _

6. sots   _ (_) _ _

7. grwino   (_) _ _ _ _

8. mcibl   (_) _ _ _

9. kera   _ _ _ (_)

Fill in the Blank

Now use the circled letters above to fill in the right answers below!

_ _ _ _ occurs whenever a _ _ _ _ _ moves an object to a new location.

Classify Energy

Identify the following energy examples as either chemical, thermal, or mechanical. The first one is done for you.

ENERGY EXAMPLES	THERMAL	CHEMICAL	MECHANICAL
1. The reaction of sugar and oxygen in the process of respiration		✓	
2. The reaction of sulfur, charcoal, and potassium nitrate in exploding fireworks			
3. Wheels turning on a bicycle			
4. The movement of a pair of scissors			
5. A hot oven			
6. Throwing a ball			
7. A mug of hot cocoa			
8. Skipping rope			
9. A warm bath			
10. The reaction of baking soda and vinegar			

Chapter 4

Energy Transformation

Fill in the blanks to complete the sentences.

1. Robinson Crusoe starts a fire by rubbing two sticks together. He is converting mechanical energy into .... energy.

2. Hawkeye pulls the trigger of Killdeer, his beloved rifle. The sulfur, charcoal, and potassium nitrate in the gunpowder react with each other and explode, driving a bullet out of the gun. Hawkeye has just converted chemical energy into .... energy.

3. Mary Anne, Mike Mulligan's steam shovel, heats steam to power her shovel as she digs the foundation for the town hall. She is converting thermal energy into .... energy.

4. Shivering in the blizzard, Charles Ingalls, Laura's Pa, converts mechanical energy into .... energy.

5. Chitty Chitty Bang Bang, a gasoline-powered car, converts chemical energy into .... energy.

6. The rising hot-air balloon of Phileas Fogg—the man famous for travelling around the world in eighty days—converts thermal energy into .... energy.

7. Jumping up and down, Nick converts the chemical energy in his cells into .... energy.

8. The burning wood-fire in King Arthur's great hall converts chemical energy into .... energy.

Potential and Kinetic Energy

Identify whether the following have potential or kinetic energy. Write "potential" or "kinetic" in the space provided.

1. A ball held in the air ....

2. An acorn as it falls from the tree to the ground ....

3. The gasoline in the tank of a parked car ....

4. A bird flying through the air ....

5. Water at the top of a waterfall ....

6. Bubbling baking soda and vinegar ....

7. An exploding firecracker ....

8. An unlit match ....

9. Nick and Christie playing hopscotch ....

Design your own roller coaster:
https://www.learner.org/series/interactive-amusement-park-physics/

Chapter 4

The Sensation of Heat and Conduction

Fill in the blanks to complete the sentences.

1. .... always moves from an object that is hotter to an object that is colder.

2. When an object feels hot or cold to you, it's because your fingers detect that .... is entering or leaving your body.

3. The transfer of thermal energy through atoms and molecules bumping into each other is called ....

4. No transfer of thermal energy will occur through conduction unless the objects are ....

5. Materials that are particularly good at "passing on" thermal energy are called .... One example is ....

6. Materials that don't "pass on" thermal energy very well are called .... One example is ....

The sensation of heat: https://www.exploratorium.edu/snacks/cold-metal

Convection and Radiation

Fill in the blanks.

1. List the three ways in which thermal energy can be transferred:

   ....

2. Energy is spread through liquids and gases by the process of

   ....

3. Warm lemonade floats to the top of the glass because it is less .... than the cold lemonade around it.

4. When we feel the warmth from the Sun or from a hot clothes iron, we are feeling

   .... rays.

5. All .... radiate infrared rays.

6. Electromagnetic waves, including infrared rays, transfer ....

   .... by "bumping into" the molecules in objects.

7. We don't notice the energy radiated by an ice cube because

   ....

Chapter 4

Chapter 4 Review

Use complete sentences to answer the following questions.

1. What is energy?

2. What is the scientific definition of work?

3. What is mechanical energy?

4. What is thermal energy?

5. What is chemical energy?

6. What is potential energy?

7. What is kinetic energy?

8. What is conduction?

   ....
   ....
   ....

9. What are insulators and conductors?

   ....
   ....
   ....

10. What is convection?

    ....
    ....
    ....

11. What is radiation?

    ....
    ....
    ....

12. What are infrared rays?

    ....
    ....
    ....

13. List at least three types of electromagnetic waves.

    ....
    ....
    ....

Chapter 5

Fill in the Blanks

Fill in the blanks to complete the sentences.

1. Atoms are made of .... , ... , and ....

2. .... are at the heart of static electricity.

3. .... refers to the build-up of electrons (negative charge) on objects.

4. Normally, the atoms making up a substance contain the same number of electrons as ....

5. When a balloon is negatively charged, it has more .... than ....

6. When a balloon is positively charged, it has more .... than ....

7. Unlike charges .... and like charges ....

8. When "extra" electrons in a negatively charged object "jump" through the air into another object, we call the event a ....

9. Electrons can't travel through the .... , but they can travel through ....

CHECK IT OUT!

Static electricity videos: https://education.jlab.org/frost/

Sparker: https://www.exploratorium.edu/science_explorer/sparker.html

What Is True?

Mark "T" if the statement is true; mark "F" if the statement is false.

1. .... Three non-magnetic materials are glass, iron, and wood.

2. .... Whenever magnetic materials are placed near a magnet, they start acting like magnets themselves; this is called static electricity.

3. .... If you bring the north pole of one magnet near the south pole of another magnet, the two magnets will repel each other.

4. .... Scientists have discovered that electricity and magnetism are a single force.

5. .... There is no way to predict how a magnet will attract or repel another object.

6. .... A magnetic field is one of the regions in northern Greece where magnets were first discovered.

7. .... An electric field is the region in which the "push" or "pull" of an electron or proton can be felt by other particles.

8. .... Electric fields and magnetic fields look exactly the same.

9. The figure to the right shows a proton placed between the balloon and the ceiling. Draw an arrow in the empty circle to show in what direction the proton will move. Remember, like charges repel and opposite charges attract.

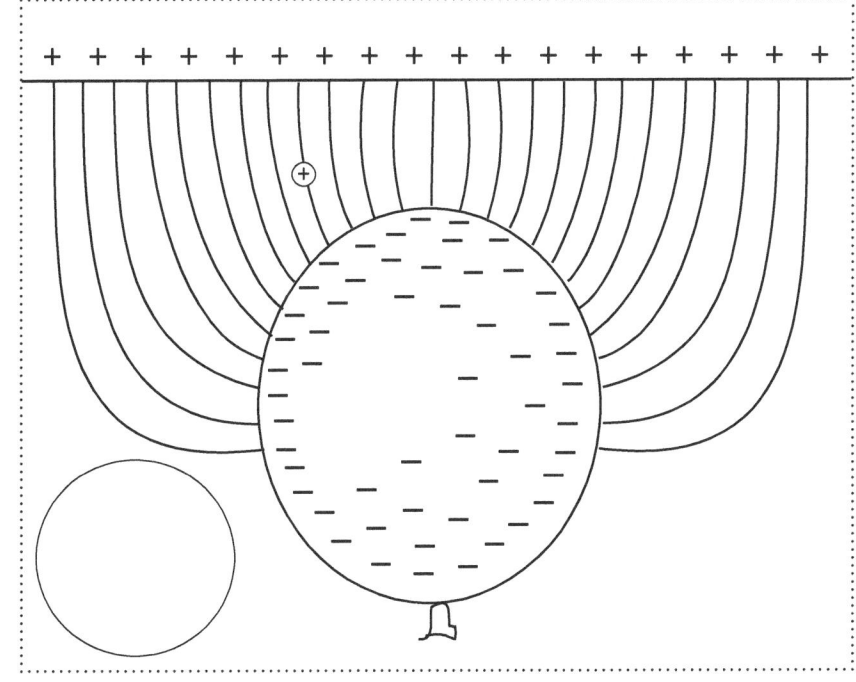

CHECK IT OUT!

Magnetic fields: https://www.exploratorium.edu/snacks/magnetic-lines-of-force

Chapter 5

Fill in the Blanks

Can you fill in the missing words?

1. At this point in the cycle, the water has .... energy.

2. At this point in the cycle, the water has .... energy.

3. When the water is calm, it has .... energy.

4. By pushing the water up to a higher position, the pump gives it .... energy.

An .... is the flow of millions of electrons through an
     5.
electrical wire. .... in a wire will just sit still or move aimlessly if they are
                 6.
left to themselves. But when a battery or a .... gives them energy, they
                                              7.
can turn a fan or light a bulb. Once the electric .... has passed through
                                                  8.
the light bulb, it no longer possesses much .... The .... would
                                             9.   10.
just sit around like the water in the pond at this point, except that the ....
                                                                          11.
or .... pump is "sucking" them back along the wire.
   12.

Chapter 5

More about Electricity

Fill in the blanks to complete the sentences.

1. ……………………… ……………………… ……………………… is a difference in charge between two materials.

2. Batteries and generators generally have one positive end filled with ……………………… and one negative end filled with ……………………… .

3. The ……………………… between the two sides of a battery or generator provides the "push" that keeps the electrons moving.

4. When the two ends of a ……………………… or ……………………… are connected by a wire, the electrons in the negative end "push" against the electrons in the wire because they want to get closer to the protons in the positive end.

5. The "push" of electrical energy travels down the wire in less than a second, but the electrons themselves move very ……………………… .

6. If we get electrical energy out of one end of a wire, we know that there was ……………………… done on the other end to provide us with this energy.

7. The Law of Conservation of Energy states that we can't get ……………………… for ……………………… .

8. One ……………………… is equal to the charge of six billion, billion electrons (six quintillion or 6,000,000,000,000,000,000).

9. The ……………………… is a unit that tells us how many electrons are going past a certain point every second.

10. The term ……………………… is used to measure the strength of the "push" that a generator or battery gives to an electric current.

Chapter 5   25

Chapter 5 Review

Answer in complete sentences.

1. What is the most important fact about charges?

   ....

   ....

2. After Nick left the tunnel slide, why did his hair keep standing on end?

   ....

   ....

   ....

3. What is induced magnetism?

   ....

   ....

   ....

4. What is a magnetic field?

   ....

   ....

   ....

5. What is an electric field?

   ....

   ....

   ....

6. What is an electric current?

   ....

   ....

   ....

7. What is an electrical potential difference?

   ....
   ....
   ....

8. How quickly do electrons move in an ordinary wire?

   ....
   ....
   ....

9. How quickly does the push of energy from a generator or battery move through a wire?

   ....
   ....
   ....

10. What does the Law of Conservation of Energy state?

    ....
    ....
    ....

11. What does the term "watt" measure? Choose an electrical appliance in your house and figure out how many watts it uses.

    ....
    ....
    ....

CHECK IT OUT!

Lemon battery: http://hilaroad.com/camp/projects/lemon/lemon_battery.html
Vinegar battery: http://hilaroad.com/camp/projects/lemon/vinegar_battery.html
Stripped-down motor: https://www.exploratorium.edu/snacks/stripped-down-motor?activity=138
Stripped-down motor 2: http://hilaroad.com/camp/projects/magnet.html

Can you match the terms on the left with their definitions or examples on the right?

12. .... magnet

13. .... static electricity

14. .... electrons

15. .... non-magnetic materials

16. .... static electrical discharge

17. .... batteries and generators

18. .... coulomb

19. .... volt

a. particles that are constantly whizzing around the nucleus of an atom

b. the jump of extra electrons in a negatively-charged object through the air into another object

c. a piece of metal that can attract, or pull, other metals

d. term that measures how much charge an object has

e. the build up of electrons (negative charge) on objects

f. copper, glass, paper, and wood

g. term that measures the "push" that a generator or battery gives to an electric current

h. "electron pumps"

Chapter 6

What Is True?

Mark "T" if the statement is true; mark "F" if the statement is false.

1. .... The six simple machines are the screw, the inclined plane, the pulley, the lever, the wheel and axle, and the hammer.

2. .... The screw-top lid on a gallon of milk is a type of simple machine.

3. .... An inclined plane allows us to fly from Los Angeles to New York in little or no time.

4. .... The screw is a special type of pulley.

5. .... Screws can convert a horizontal, rotational movement into a vertical movement; wedges can convert a vertical movement into a horizontal movement.

6. .... Whether you use an inclined plane or not, it always takes the same amount of force to raise an object three feet.

7. .... An inclined plane allows us to exert the necessary force all at once instead of little by little.

8. *Identify examples of inclined planes, screws, and wedges in your home and neighborhood. Use the space below to list two examples of each.*

   Inclined plane: ....
   Screw: ....
   Wedge: ....

Fill in the Blanks

Fill in the blanks to complete the sentences.

1. A lever is a long board or rod that rotates around a ....

2. When you press down on one side of the lever in this diagram, the other end of the lever moves ....

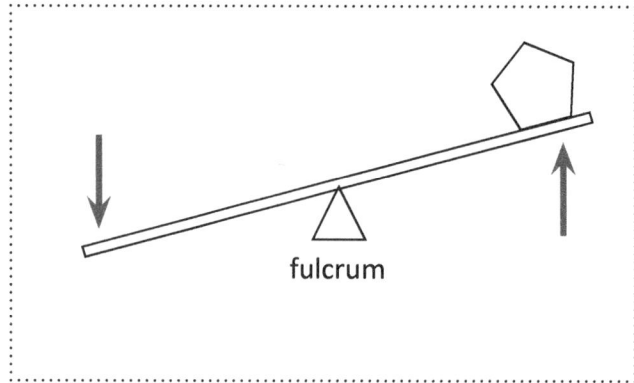

3. A teeter-totter makes it easier to lift a friend because it changes the .... of your force.

4. *Circle the correct word:* The [closer / farther] the fulcrum is to the load, the easier it is to lift the load.

5. Levers do not actually produce more force. We must either use a .... force over a short distance, or a small force over a .... distance.

6. Whenever a lever converts a large force into a small force, it is also converting a short .... into a long ....

First, Second, and Third Class Levers

Label the force, the load, and the fulcrum for the following levers.

1.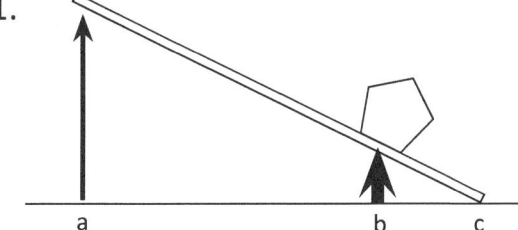

   a. ....

   b. ....

   c. ....

2.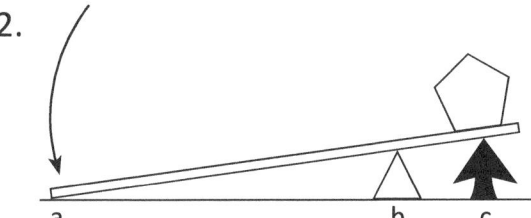

   a. ....

   b. ....

   c. ....

3.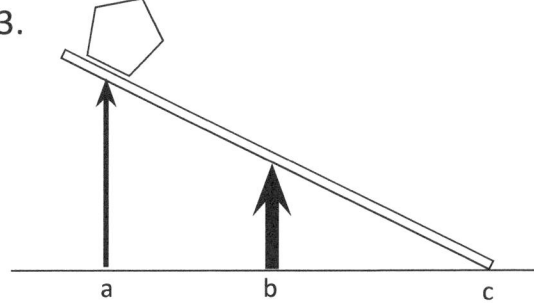

   a. ....

   b. ....

   c. ....

Chapter 6

What Is True?

Mark "T" if the statement is true; mark "F" if the statement is false.

1. .... There are three types of levers.

2. .... In first class levers, the fulcrum is always between the force and the load.

3. .... A broom is an example of a first class lever.

4. .... Second class levers multiply force and change its direction.

5. .... A wheelbarrow is an example of a second class lever.

6. .... Third class levers multiply distance without changing the direction of the force.

7. .... In a fishing pole, the fulcrum is at one end, the load is at the other end, and the force is in the middle.

8. .... A fishing pole is an example of a second class lever.

9. .... If we want to change the direction of a force, we could use a first class lever or a second class lever.

Science Notebook

Draw diagrams of a first class lever, a second class lever, and a third class lever in your Science Notebook. Be sure to label the force, fulcrum, and load in each diagram. Next to each diagram, list as many examples as you can of each type of lever. Challenge your family to think of even more examples!

Wheels Make Work Easier

Fill in the blanks to complete the sentences.

1. .... is the "drag" that we feel when we move objects across each other.

2. A .... makes our work easier because, as the wheel turns, no one part of the wheel touches the ground for more than an instant at a time.

3. When a wheel is firmly attached to a rod or smaller wheel, it becomes a simple machine called the ....

4. If you twist a wheel and axle and the wheel makes a full turn, then the axle makes a .... turn.

5. You can do the same amount of .... by turning the axle as you can by turning the wheel.

6. It is easier to turn the handle of a screwdriver than to twist its neck because the handle spreads your force over a longer ....

7. In a .... wheel-and-axle system, force is applied to the axle instead of to the wheel.

8. A reverse wheel and axle multiplies ...., but it does not multiply force.

Miracle staircase: https://www.lorettochapel.com/info/staircase

Chapter 6

Wheels

Label each example below as a rolling wheel or a wheel and axle. Ask yourself if the wheel is being used to reduce friction or to multiply force/distance.

1. Door knob ....

2. Electric fan ....

3. Wheels on a wheel chair ....

4. Wheels on a vacuum cleaner ....

5. Screwdriver ....

6. Helicopter propeller ....

7. Wheels on a skateboard ....

8. Ferris wheel ....

Science Notebook

Write two headers at the top of a page: "Rolling wheel" and "Wheel and axle." Under each header list as many examples as you can of those types of wheels. Challenge your family to think of even more examples!

Pulleys

Fill in the blanks to complete the sentences.

1. Figure A is a .... pulley.

2. Figure B is a .... pulley.

3. A fixed pulley reverses the .... of a force.

4. A moveable pulley .... force.

5. In Figure C, Mike uses one moveable pulley and one fixed pulley. In Figure D, Mike uses two moveable pulleys and one fixed pulley. Mike has to use the most force in Figure .... Mike has to pull the rope farthest in Figure ....

True or False? Mark "T" if the statement is true; mark "F" if the statement is false.

6. .... Mike can multiply a force and reverse the direction of a force by combining a fixed pulley and a moveable pulley.

7. .... If Mike used enough fixed pulleys, he could even lift an elephant.

8. .... Pulleys can only multiply force by increasing distance.

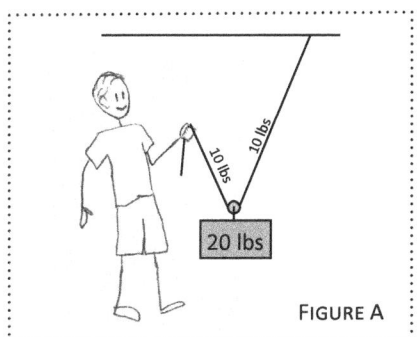

FIGURE A

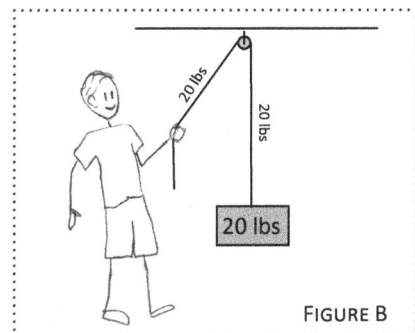

FIGURE B

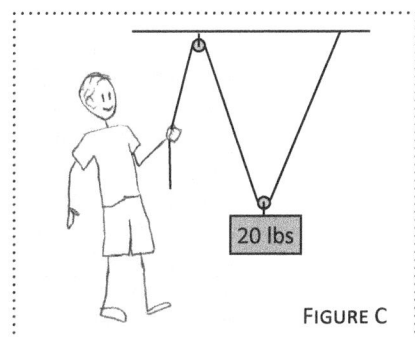

FIGURE C

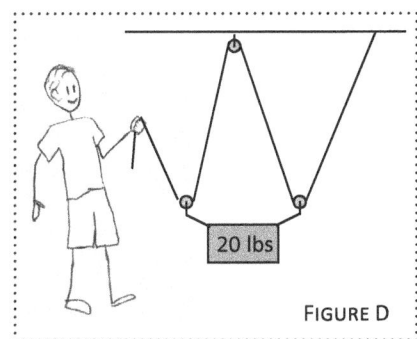

FIGURE D

Chapter 6

Chapter 6 Review

Answer in complete sentences.

1. What is an inclined plane?

2. What is a screw?

3. What is a wedge?

4. What is a lever?

5. What is a wheel and axle?

6. What is a pulley?

7. What is a fixed pulley?

8. What is a moveable pulley?
   ....
   ....

9. What is a fulcrum?
   ....
   ....

10. What is friction?
    ....
    ....

*Cross out the example that does **not** match the word.*

11. **Inclined Plane:**	stairs	crowbar	twisting mountain roads
12. **Screw:**	tongs	screws	screw-top lid
13. **Wedge:**	hatchet	nail	crowbar
14. **Lever:**	teeter-totter	stairs	fishing pole
15. **First Class Lever:**	teeter-totter	crowbar	broom
16. **Second Class Lever:**	hammer	wheelbarrow	nutcracker
17. **Third Class Lever:**	oars	fishing pole	tennis racket
18. **Wheel and axle:**	screwdriver	ferris wheel	nail

Unit 1 Test

Multiple choice: Circle the correct answer.

1. The amount of matter that is in an object is its

    a. volume   b. mass   c. magnetic field

2. Gravity

    a. doesn't act on empty space   b. is a force that acts on volume

    c. is the measurement of how much matter is packed into a certain space

3. When an object is less dense than water, the buoyant force makes it

    a. float   b. sink   c. dissolve   d. explode

4. Atoms are made of

    a. proteins and nutrients   b. protons, electrons, and neutrons

    c. small particles called nuclei

5. Matter expands when it is

    a. heated   b. cooled   c. dissolved

6. Vaporization is the process of turning a

    a. gas into a solid   b. solid into a liquid   c. liquid into a gas

7. Solvent is the scientific name for

    a. "dissolved"   b. "dissolver"   c. "solution"   d. the answer

8. *Fill in the blank:* .... is the ability to do work.

    a. Force   b. Hopscotch   c. Energy   d. Strength

9. Which of the following is an example of potential energy?

    a. playing basketball   b. holding a ball above one's head

    c. baking soda reacting with vinegar

10. The most important thing to remember about positive and negative charges is:

    a. Unlike charges attract and like charges repel.
    b. Unlike poles attract and like poles repel.
    c. One has a good attitude and one does not.
    d. Unlike charges repel and like charges attract.

11. The region in which a magnet's "pull" can be felt by magnetic materials is called its

    a. induced magnetism   b. magnetic field   c. invisible force

12. All electrical equipment is powered by a flow of .... passed from electron to electron.

    a. water   b. density   c. energy

13. *Circle as many as apply:* Simple machines include:

    a. ramp   b. nail   c. shoe   d. cup

14. *Fill in the blank:* A .... lever is one in which the force is at one end, the load is at the other, and the fulcrum is in the middle.

    a. first class   b. second class   c. third class

15. A fixed pulley ....

    a. changes the direction of a force   b. multiplies force   c. needs no repairs

Unit 1

Relationships

Label the following examples as parasitic, facilitative, or predatory. If the example is parasitic or predatory, label the predator and prey, or parasite and host. The first one is done for you.

   predator prey
1. cat : parakeet = *predatory relationship*

2. fish : grizzly bear = ...

3. honey bee : daffodil = ...

4. mosquito : rabbit = ...

5. snake : frog = ...

6. squirrel : oak tree = ...

7. frog : butterfly = ...

Science Notebook

Add to your Science Notebook a parasitic, a facilitative, and a predatory relationship that were not mentioned above. If the example is parasitic or predatory, label the predator and prey, or parasite and host.

Food Chains

Fill in the blanks using words from the word bank to build two food chains below.

1. .... top predator

   .... secondary consumer

   .... primary consumer

   ......*algae*............... primary producer

2. .... top predator

   .... primary consumer

   ......*bush*............... primary producer

WORD BANK

kingfisher

deer

trout

tadpole

mountain lion

Fill in the blanks.

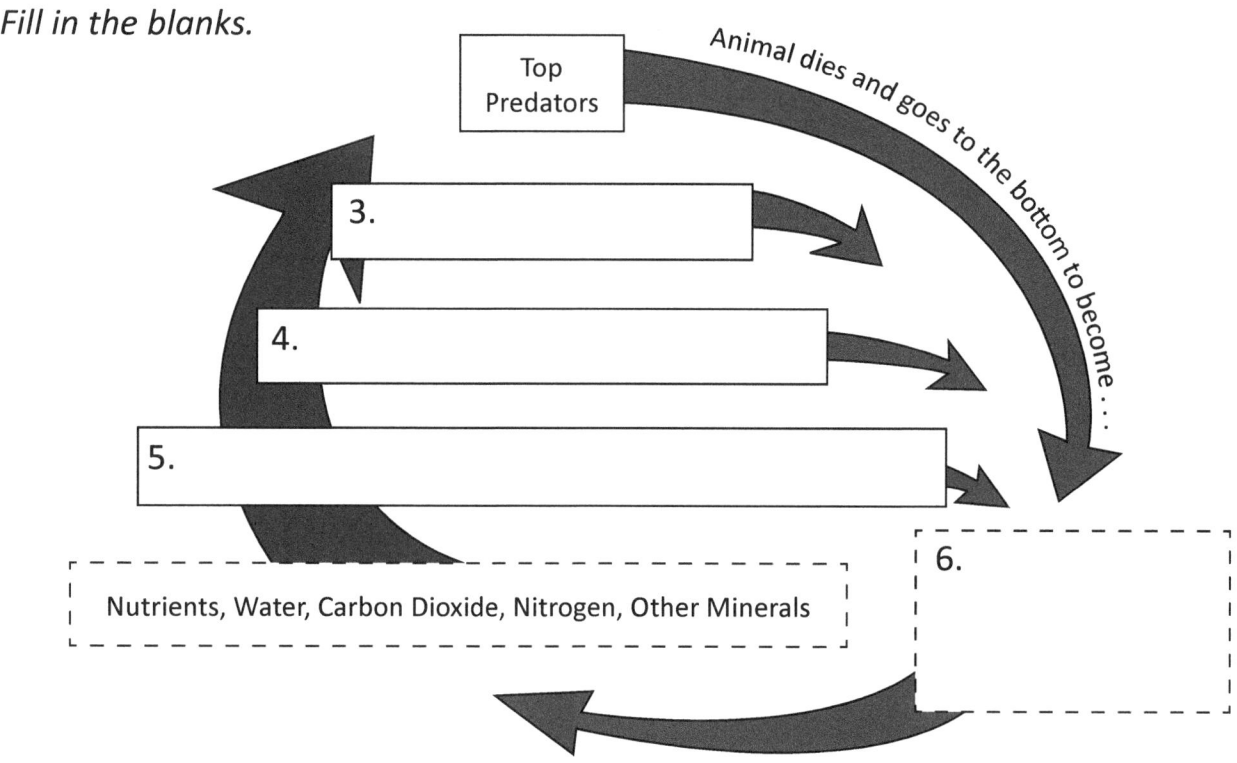

Nutrients, Water, Carbon Dioxide, Nitrogen, Other Minerals

CHECK IT OUT!

Animal movies: https://www.exploringnature.org/db/view/693
Tracking sunlight: https://journeynorth.org/mclass/
Bottle biology: http://bottlebiology.org/investigations/decomp_main.html

Biomes Map

Circle the correct answer. Refer to the Biomes Map on page 119 in your textbook when necessary.

1. In which climate zone do you live?

    a. South Polar   b. South Temperate   c. South Tropical

    d. North Tropical   e. North Temperate   f. North Polar

2. The boreal forest can be found mainly in the ………… Zone.

    a. South Polar   b. South Temperate   c. North Temperate   d. North Tropical

3. The North and South Tropical Zones are separated by the ………… .

    a. Tropic of Capricorn   b. Equator   c. Arctic Circle

4. Tropical grassland can be found mainly in the North and South ………… Zones.

    a. Polar   b. Temperate   c. Tropical

5. There are deserts in every part of the globe except the

    a. polar zones   b. temperate zones   c. tropical zones

6. According to the Biomes Map, which biome *cannot* be found in Australia?

    a. temperate grassland   b. desert   c. tropical grassland   d. boreal forest

7. Which biome *cannot* be found in the United States or Canada?

    a. temperate grassland   b. desert   c. tropical grassland   d. tundra

8. Which type of forest *cannot* be found in Africa?

    a. temperate forest   b. tropical forest   c. boreal forest

Chapter 7

Match-Up

Choose the best definition to match the terms on the left.

1. .... species
2. .... habitat
3. .... niche
4. .... ecology
5. .... interdependent
6. .... biomes
7. .... primary producer
8. .... primary consumer
9. .... top predator
10. .... photosynthesis
11. .... chemosynthesis
12. .... organic material
13. .... Equator
14. .... latitude lines

A. The last link and strongest animal in the food chain

B. The special role a species plays in a biome

C. The process by which deep-sea bacteria use chemicals to convert nutrients and minerals into food energy

D. The process by which plants and algae use sunlight to convert nutrients and minerals into food energy

E. Types of plants and animals

F. When creatures depend on each other for survival

G. Material that is or was part of a living creature. Leaves, bones, feathers, and scat are examples.

H. A creature that converts non-living nutrients and minerals into food energy

I. Imaginary, horizontal lines marking a location's distance above or below the Equator.

J. The area in which an animal lives

K. Major regions of the globe, each with its own unique climate and its own community of plants and animals

L. A creature that gets its energy by eating the food energy stored in the stems, leaves, and fruit of the primary producer

M. An imaginary line around the center of the globe, at an equal distance from the North and South Poles

N. The type of biology that explores how the different parts of Creation—plants, animals, weather, terrain—work together

CHECK IT OUT!

Animal sounds: https://animaldiversity.org/site/accounts/sounds/Animalia.html

Food chains and interdependence: https://www.learner.org/wp-content/interactive/envsci/ecology/ecology.html

Chapter 8

Tundra Profile

Create a "profile page" for the tundra biome in your Science Notebook. Be sure to include the following information, as well as anything else you particularly wish to remember about this biome. Feel free to decorate the page with original illustrations, pictures clipped from magazines, etc. All the required information can be found in the textbook, but you may need to wait until the end of the chapter to learn some of the facts.

1. Summer and winter temperatures
2. Hours of daylight in summer
3. Hours of daylight in winter
4. Length of growing season
5. Average annual precipitation
6. A short description of the soil, climate, and plant and animal species that live in the tundra
7. Would you like to live in the tundra? Why or why not?

Tundra Research Assignment

Research tardigrades, also known as water bears or moss piglets. Share your findings with your family. Be prepared to explain how other creatures survive in the tundra.

Animals: https://www.exploringnature.org/db/animals
Tracking migration: https://journeynorth.org/
Arctic photos: https://www.arcticphoto.com/
Lichen: http://www.sharnoffphotos.com/lichens/lichens_home_index.html
Polar regions: https://www.exploringnature.org/db/view/Polar-Regions

Thinking about the Chapter, Part 1

Answer the questions in complete sentences.

1. Why are tundra days 24 hours long in the summer?

   ....

   ....

   ....

2. Why can't trees grow in the tundra?

   ....

   ....

   ....

3. Briefly describe the winter habitat of lemmings.

   ....

   ....

   ....

4. Why don't most tundra animals hibernate during the winter?

   ....

   ....

   ....

5. How do freeze-avoidant insects survive the winter?

   ....

   ....

   ....

Relationships and Food Chains

Label the following examples as parasitic, facilitative, or predatory. If the example is parasitic or predatory, label the predator and prey, or parasite and host.

1. seal : polar bear = ...

2. caribou : mosquito = ...

3. mountain avens : insects = ...

4. snowy owl : rock ptarmigan = ...

5. caribou : bacteria in their stomach = ...

6. mosquitoes : insect-eating birds = ...

Fill in the blanks to complete the food chains below:

7. .... : lemming : ....
       primary producer   top predator

8. lichen : .... : mosquitoes : .... : arctic fox
                primary consumer   consumer

Science Notebook

Add to your Science Notebook two other relationships from the tundra that were not mentioned above. If the example is parasitic or predatory, label the predator and prey, or parasite and host.

Chapter 8

Thinking about the Chapter, Part 2

Answer in complete sentences.

1. Why are tundra plants so short?

   ....
   ....
   ....

2. What is the length of the growing season where you live?

   ....
   ....
   ....

3. Why can caribou digest lichen when most other animals cannot?

   ....
   ....
   ....
   ....

4. Explain how lichen is an example of a facilitative relationship.

   ....
   ....
   ....
   ....

Chapter 8 Review

Mark "T" if the statement is true; mark "F" if the statement is false.

1. .... Baby muskoxen are born without any fur at all, so muskoxen do not give birth until the last snows have melted.

2. .... Freeze-tolerant insects can survive being frozen.

3. .... Some arctic plants can live for hundreds of years, growing only a tiny amount each year.

4. .... Polar bear hairs and snow are good insulators because they are full of water.

5. .... The cell membrane is the outer layer of a plant or animal cell.

6. .... The arctic tern is one of the few birds that remains in the tundra all year instead of migrating.

7. .... Polar bears usually eat only the energy-rich blubber of the seals they kill.

8. .... All plants need seeds to reproduce.

9. .... Yeast is a type of algae.

10. .... Lichen is the main food of muskoxen, arctic foxes, and polar bears.

11. .... In the tundra, the ground never thaws completely.

12. .... The reason the tundra is covered with pools of water during the summer is that it receives much more rain and snow than most biomes.

Chapter 9

Boreal Forest Profile

Create a "profile page" for the boreal forest biome in your Science Notebook. Be sure to include the following information, as well as anything else you particularly wish to remember about the biome. Feel free to decorate the page with original illustrations, pictures clipped from magazines, etc. All the required information can be found in the textbook, but you may need to wait until the end of the chapter to learn some of the facts.

1. Summer and winter temperatures
2. Hours of daylight in summer
3. Hours of daylight in winter
4. Are boreal forest summers longer or shorter than tundra summers?
5. Average annual precipitation
6. A short description of the soil, climate, and plant and animal species that live in the boreal forest
7. Would you like to live in the boreal forest? Why or why not?

Boreal Forest Research Assignment

Choose one or more of the following to research: porcupine, wood frog, grizzly bear, muskrat, Northern flying squirrel, Canada goose. Share your findings with your family. You can model your report after Dani's beaver report on pgs. 152-155 of the text.

Alaska wildlife: http://www.adfg.alaska.gov/index.cfm?adfg=animals.main

Wetlands of the world: https://www.exploringnature.org/db/view/Wetlands-of-the-World

Thinking about the Chapter, Part 1

Answer the questions in complete sentences.

1. Why is the soil in the boreal forest so poor?

   ....

   ....

   ....

   ....

2. Explain the differences between a bog (muskeg) and a fen.

   ....

   ....

   ....

   ....

3. How do beavers build their lodges?

   ....

   ....

   ....

   ....

4. Where do beavers get their food in the winter?

   ....

   ....

   ....

   ....

Relationships and Food Chains

Label the following examples as parasitic, facilitative, or predatory. If the example is parasitic or predatory, label the predator and prey, or parasite and host.

1. fisher : porcupine = ...

2. beaver : fish and frogs living in the beaver pond = ...

3. jack pine : jack pine budworms = ...

4. sundew : insect = ...

5. salmon : grizzly bear = ...

Fill in the blanks to complete the food chains below:

6. leaves and moss : snowshoe hare : ....
                                                                           top predator

7. .... : red crossbill : fisher
    primary producer

Science Notebook

Add to your Science Notebook two other relationships from the boreal forest that were not mentioned above. If the example is parasitic or predatory, label the predator and prey, or parasite and host.

Thinking about the Chapter, Part 2

Answer in complete sentences.

1. Describe at least three ways in which evergreen conifers are better equipped to grow in the boreal forest than deciduous trees are.

2. Describe three ways in which fire can be good for a forest.

3. Why do carnivorous plants capture insects?

4. Briefly describe the life cycle of a salmon.

Chapter 9

Chapter 9 Review

Mark "T" if the statement is true; mark "F" if the statement is false.

1. .... Beavers store most of their fat in their tails.

2. .... Deciduous trees are trees that remain green all year round.

3. .... The snow can be 10-12 feet deep in the boreal forest.

4. .... Pine needles are better than broad leaves at conserving water.

5. .... Salmon spend most of their lives in the ocean.

6. .... Bladderworts use their sticky tentacles to capture insects.

7. .... The boreal forest, also known as the taiga, is the largest of all land biomes.

8. .... The inside of a beaver lodge stays at about 75°F all year round.

9. .... Newly-hatched salmon are called salmon fry.

10. .... Caribou live in the boreal forest in the summer, but they migrate to the tundra during the winter.

11. .... Jack pine cones only open when they are exposed to the heat of a fire.

12. .... Fens are more treacherous than bogs.

13. .... The largest salmon ever caught weighed 126 pounds.

14. .... The resin in conifers is quite flammable.

15. .... Anadromous fish return to freshwater streams to lay their eggs.

Chapter 10

Temperate Forest Profile

Create a "profile page" for the temperate forest biome in your Science Notebook. Be sure to include the following information, as well as anything else you particularly wish to remember about this biome. Feel free to decorate the page with original illustrations, pictures clipped from magazines, etc. All the required information can be found in the textbook, but you may need to wait until the end of the chapter to learn some of the facts.

1. Summer and winter temperatures

2. Type and length of seasons

3. Average annual precipitation

4. A short description of the soil, climate, and plant and animal species that live in the temperate forest

5. Would you like to live in the temperate forest? Why or why not?

Forests of the world: https://www.exploringnature.org/db/view/Forests-of-the-World
Rainforest sounds: https://www.exploratorium.edu/frogs/rainforest/index.html
Rainforests of the world: https://www.exploringnature.org/db/view/Rainforests-of-the-World

Tropical Rainforest Profile

Create a "profile page" for the tropical rainforest biome in your Science Notebook. Be sure to include the following information, as well as anything else you particularly wish to remember about the biome. Feel free to decorate the page with original illustrations, pictures clipped from magazines, etc. All the required information can be found in the textbook, but you may need to wait until the end of the chapter to learn some of the facts.

1. Summer and winter temperatures
2. Type and length of seasons
3. Length of day in summer and in winter (see Introduction to Biomes 7.3)
4. Average annual precipitation
5. A short description of the soil, climate, and plant and animal species that live in the tropical rainforest
6. Would you like to live in the tropical rainforest? Why or why not?
7. What percentage of the world's species is contained in tropical forests?
8. Sketch the layers of the rainforest and draw some of the animals that can be found in each.

Temperate Forest or Rainforest Research Assignment

Research an animal from either the temperate forest or the rainforest. Choose one or more of the following animals to research:

Temperate forest: Eastern box turtle, spotted salamander, red panda, koala, kiwi bird

Rainforest: Malaysian flying frog, mudskipper, glasswinged butterfly, electric eel, pangolin, army ant

Share your findings with your family. You can model your report after Dani's beaver report on pgs. 152-155 of the text.

Thinking about the Chapter, Part 1

Answer the questions in complete sentences.

1. Why are there hardly any reptiles and amphibians in the tundra and boreal forest?

   ....
   ....
   ....
   ....

2. Why does the temperature in the rainforest remain the same throughout the year?

   ....
   ....
   ....
   ....

3. Why is the soil in tropical rainforests so poor?

   ....
   ....
   ....
   ....

4. Why do small rainforest plants grow in the branches of trees instead of on the forest floor?

   ....
   ....
   ....
   ....

Chapter 10

Relationships and Food Chains

Label the following examples as parasitic, facilitative, or predatory. If the example is parasitic or predatory, label the predator and prey, or parasite and host.

1. *Cecropia* tree : ants = ...

2. jaguar : Brazilian tapir = ...

3. sloth : algae = ...

4. strangler fig : tree = ...

5. arowana : insect = ...

6. pollinating moth : flower = ...

7. giant anteater : ants = ...

Fill in the blanks to complete the food chains below:

8. fruit : .... : ....
                 primary consumer   top predator

9. brazil nut : .... : ocelot
                 primary consumer

Science Notebook

Add to your Science Notebook two other relationships from the temperate forest or rainforest that were not mentioned above. If the example is parasitic or predatory, label the predator and prey, or parasite and host.

Thinking about the Chapter, Part 2

Answer the questions in complete sentences.

1. Why is there more undergrowth on the edge of rivers and clearings than there is deep in the rainforest?

   ....
   ....
   ....
   ....

2. How are so many species able to live and flourish in the rainforest?

   ....
   ....
   ....
   ....

3. Describe at least three examples of specialization in the rainforest.

   ....
   ....
   ....
   ....

4. Describe at least three examples of camouflage in the rainforest.

   ....
   ....
   ....
   ....

Chapter 10 Review

Mark "T" if the statement is true; mark "F" if the statement is false.

1. .... The rainforest has fewer insects than the tundra does.

2. .... The *Cecropia* tree grows packages of food for the ants that live in its hollow branches.

3. .... In the temperate forest, the year is divided into two seasons: wet and dry.

4. .... The Amazon River floods its banks every year.

5. .... Some bromeliads can hold up to two tons of water.

6. .... The main challenge for rainforest plants is getting enough sunlight.

7. .... The crested green basilisk lizard can leap three feet into the air to catch insects off of low-hanging leaves.

8. .... Some pythons have heat-sensitive pits on their noses that allow them to track down prey by detecting its body heat.

9. .... Poison dart frogs can change their skin color to blend in with their surroundings.

10. .... Tropical rainforests contain about 7% of the plant, animal, and insect species in the world.

11. .... Some rainforests are perpetually shrouded in clouds and mists, and there are others that are flooded under 30 feet of water for much of the year.

12. .... Epiphytes are plants that grow on large boulders.

13. .... The emergent layer of the rainforest is the layer just below the canopy.

14. .... Deer, peccaries, and agoutis are at home in the understory of the rainforest.

15. .... A niche is the special role that a species plays in a biome.

Chapter 11

Temperate and Tropical Grassland Profile

Create two "profile pages" in your Science Notebook, one for the temperate grassland biome and one for the tropical grassland biome. Be sure to include the following information on each profile page, as well as anything else you particularly wish to remember about this biome. Feel free to decorate the pages with original illustrations, pictures clipped from magazines, etc. All the required information can be found in the textbook, but you may need to wait until the end of the chapter to learn some of the facts.

1. Summer and winter temperatures

2. Type and length of seasons

3. Average annual precipitation

4. A short description of the soil, climate, and plant and animal species that live in the temperate/tropical grassland

5. Would you like to live in the temperate/tropical grassland? Why or why not?

CHECK IT OUT!
Grasslands of the world: https://www.exploringnature.org/db/view/Grasslands-of-the-World
Deserts of the world: https://www.exploringnature.org/db/view/Deserts-of-the-World
Mountains of the world: https://www.exploringnature.org/db/view/Mountains-of-the-World
Oceans of the world: https://www.exploringnature.org/db/view/Oceans-of-the-World

Thinking about the Chapter, Part 1

Answer the questions in complete sentences.

1. What are the two reasons that very few trees grow on the prairie?

   ....
   ....
   ....
   ....

2. Why is the dung beetle important to life in the African savanna?

   ....
   ....
   ....
   ....

3. Why are termites important in the African savanna? Give a few examples of the uses that animals make of termite mounds.

   ....
   ....
   ....
   ....
   ....
   ....

Desert Profile

Create a "profile page" for the desert biome in your Science Notebook. Be sure to include the following information, as well as anything else you particularly wish to remember about this biome. Feel free to decorate the page with original illustrations, pictures clipped from magazines, etc. All the required information can be found in the textbook, but you may need to wait until the end of the chapter to learn some of the facts.

1. Daytime and nighttime temperatures

2. Does the growing season occur in the summer or in the winter?

3. Average annual precipitation

4. A short description of the terrain, climate, and plant and animal species that live in the desert

5. Would you like to live in the desert? Why or why not?

Grassland or Desert Research Assignment

Research an animal from the temperate grassland, the tropical grassland, or the desert. Choose one or more of the following to research:

Temperate grassland: bison, prairie dog, Przewalski's horse, European legless lizard

Tropical grassland: Komodo dragon, cheetah, mongoose, weaverbird

Desert: Arabian oryx, ant lion, dromedary camel, sand cat

Share your findings with your family. You can model your report after Dani's beaver report on pgs. 152-155 of the text.

Relationships and Food Chains

Label the following examples as parasitic, facilitative, or predatory. If the example is parasitic or predatory, label the predator and prey, or parasite and host.

1. dung beetle : grazing animals = ...

2. snake : secretary bird = ...

3. sidewinder : lizard = ...

4. mongoose : cobra = ...

5. beetle : tarantula = ...

Fill in the blanks to complete the food chains below:

6. .... : grasshopper : .... : roadrunner : coyote
    primary producer   consumer

7. leaves : gerenuk : ....
                               top predator

Science Notebook

Add to your Science Notebook two other relationships from the prairie, the savanna, or the desert that were not mentioned above. If the example is parasitic or predatory, label the predator and prey, or parasite and host.

Thinking about the Chapter, Part 2

Answer in complete sentences.

1. How do large ears and slender bodies help desert animals to cool off?

   ....
   ....
   ....
   ....

2. Describe at least three desert animals and the techniques and equipment they have for surviving in the desert.

   ....
   ....
   ....
   ....

3. Describe the two different types of root systems in the desert, and how plants use them to obtain water.

   ....
   ....
   ....

4. Explain why it is important for seedlings to sprout at a distance from their parent plants.

   ....
   ....
   ....

Chapter 11

Chapter 11 Review

Mark "T" if the statement is true; mark "F" if the statement is false.

1. .... The temperate grasslands in South America are called pampas.

2. .... Corn is a domesticated species of grass.

3. .... The smaller an animal's ears are, the easier it is for it to stay cool in the desert.

4. .... Kangaroos, kudus, and gerenuks can be found in the African savanna.

5. .... The term "elevation" refers to a location's distance above sea-level.

6. .... Stomata are tiny holes in plants' leaves that open to take in carbon dioxide.

7. .... The African sandgrouse will fly as far as 20 miles every morning to bring water to its young.

8. .... The mongoose is a favorite prey of cobras.

9. .... Some desert animals do not have to drink at all.

10. .... In the desert, deciduous trees lose their leaves in the spring.

11. .... Many termites install electrical air-conditioning units in their mounds.

12. .... A desert could have double its normal rainfall one year, but no water at all for the next three years.

13. .... Strictly speaking, a desert is any place where the temperature remains above 100°F during the day and night.

14. .... Every place on Earth belongs to either the tundra, boreal forest, temperate forest, rainforest, prairie, savanna, or desert biome.

15. .... When animals estivate, they go into a period of summer dormancy.

16. .... Marsupials are animals that have pouches for raising their young.

Chapter 12

What Is True?

Mark "T" if the statement is true; mark "F" if the statement is false.

1. .... Swamps and bogs play the important role of cleaning and replenishing groundwater supplies.

2. .... The desert is the only biome that is completely useless to human beings.

3. .... Man has a responsibility to care for Creation.

4. .... One way that farmers care for the soil is by rotating crops.

5. .... Wise fishermen provide food for the hungry by capturing every fish in the ocean.

6. .... Northern Israel receives about 40 inches of precipitation per year.

7. .... When people redistribute water to where it is needed most, they are practicing irrigation.

8. .... The water in wells and pumps comes from small lakes.

9. .... The water in an aquifer collects between grains of sand and gravel or in holes or cracks in solid rock.

10. .... Drip irrigation helps farmers conserve water.

Science Notebook

In your Science Notebook, list as many natural resources as you can for each biome. Challenge your family to think of even more examples!

Fill in the Blanks #1

Fill in the blanks to complete the sentences.

1. The trees that are left after a moderate fire are called .... trees.

2. One way forests can become unhealthy is if human beings ...., or prevent, every single fire.

3. The trees in .... forests do not have the energy to fight off diseases and insect pests.

4. .... burns are small fires that foresters start intentionally as a way to keep forests healthy.

5. Careful .... can keep forests from filling up with too much dry fuel, which is a good way to prevent severe fires.

6. Most of the trees that are harvested from forests are turned into paper or ....

7. Resources that naturally replace themselves as they are used are called .... resources.

8. Many non-renewable resources can be ...., or used over and over.

9. Gasoline, diesel fuel, propane, jet fuel, and kerosene are made out of crude oil, also known as ....

Science Notebook

Brainstorm a list of the natural resources in your area. List them in your Science Notebook under the headings "food," "energy," "water and minerals," and "plants and animals."

Fill in the Blanks #2

Fill in the blanks to complete the sentences.

1. When Israeli dairy farmers crossed Damascus cows with Dutch bulls and Holstein-Friesian bulls, they were practicing .... breeding.

2. The bits of coded information (DNA) that tell a plant how to grow are called ....

3. When a scientist takes a gene from one plant and puts it into another plant, the result is a .... modified crop.

What Is True?

Mark "T" if the statement is true; mark "F" if the statement is false.

1. .... Conservation, the study of how to care for Creation and use natural resources wisely, is part of the study of astronomy.

2. .... The Russet Burbank potato saved thousands of lives during the Irish Potato Famine.

3. .... Scientists have developed a variety of corn that makes its own pesticide.

4. .... The Earth does not have enough natural resources to feed seven billion people.

Science Notebook

Reread the quotations from Benedict XVI's encyclical, Caritas in Veritate, *on pgs. 216, 224, 230, and 231. Choose two of the quotations and write them in your Science Notebook.*

Chapter 12

Unit 2 Test

Multiple choice: Circle the correct answer.

1. Which of the following is *not* a primary producer?
   a. deep-sea bacteria   b. cedar trees   c. mushrooms   d. algae

2. When creatures interact with and depend on each other for survival, we say they
   a. live in different habitats   b. are interdependent   c. are consumers

3. The relationship between fungi and algae in lichen is a .... relationship.
   a. parasitic   b. predatory   c. facilitative   d. lichenate

4. Which of the following is *not* a decomposer?
   a. worms   b. grass   c. fungi   d. bacteria

5. The North Polar Zone is separated from the North Temperate Zone by the ....
   a. Equator   b. Tropic of Capricorn   c. Arctic Circle   d. Antarctic Circle

6. The temperate forest receives less precipitation than ....
   a. the desert   b. the boreal forest   c. the tropical rainforest

7. Which of the following biomes does *not* have fertile soils?
   a. the temperate grassland   b. the temperate forest   c. the rainforest

8. Which of the following can *not* be found in the boreal forest?
   a. lakes   b. wetlands   c. burned forest areas   d. polar ice caps

9. The year is divided into four seasons of equal length in all of the following biomes except ....
   a. the temperate forest   b. the tropical rainforest   c. the temperate grassland

10. The year is divided into a wet and a dry season in all of the following biomes *except* ....
    a. the temperate forest   b. the tropical rainforest   c. the tropical grassland

11. In the boreal forest, evergreen conifers have an advantage over deciduous trees for all the following reasons *except* ....
    a. their pointed shape   b. their large size   c. their dark green color
    d. the fact that they have needles instead of broad leaves

12. Which of the following characteristics of the tundra is *not* caused by permafrost?
    a. the large number of mosquitoes   b. the absence of trees
    c. the pools of water that cover the ground   d. the cold winter temperatures

13. Tropical rainforests contain .... of the world's plant, animal, and insect species.
    a. 7%   b. 95%   c. 50%   d. 35%

14. The most critical resource in the rainforest for plants is ....
    a. soil   b. sunlight   c. water   d. air

15. The variety of plant and animal species in a certain biome is called its ....
    a. biodiversity   b. habitats   c. facilitation   d. interdependence

16. Termites and dung beetles are ....
    a. primary producers   b. useless insects   c. soil enrichers

17. Which of the following is *not* one of the survival techniques of desert animals?
    a. extracting water from food   b. going dormant in the winter
    c. swimming beneath the surface of the sand   d. doing a "thermal dance"

18. All of the following are non-renewable resources *except* ....
    a. coal   b. aluminum   c. trees   d. petroleum

UNIT 3

Ideally, star-gazing assignments should be completed as soon as the concepts have been covered in the text. If weather or other circumstances make this impractical, complete the assignment as soon as conveniently possible.

Activity #1
Complete after reading 13.3 in textbook.
Learn how to use a star chart. Identify Orion, Canis Major, Canis Minor, Taurus, the Pleiades, Betelgeuse, Sirius, Procyon, and Aldebaran. Memorize the names and positions of Betelgeuse, Sirius, and Procyon.

Activity #2
Complete after reading 13.7 in textbook.
Locate Ursa Minor (the Little Dipper), the Big Dipper, Cassiopeia, Polaris, Merak, and Dubhe. Memorize the names and positions of Merak and Dubhe. Learn how to use them to find Polaris.

Activity #3
Complete after reading 13.9 in textbook.
Purchase or make a star wheel and learn how to use it. (*https://www.skyandtelescope.com/observing/make-a-star-wheel/*)

Activity #4
Complete after reading 13.11 in textbook.
Learn how to find your latitude by the height of Polaris. Learn how to use Merak and Dubhe to tell time at night.

Activity #5
Complete after reading 14.4 in textbook.
In your Science Notebook, sketch the Moon in each of its phases over the course of one month. The Moon rises at different times depending on its phase, so you may want to consult an almanac to determine the most convenient time to view it.

Activity #6
Complete after reading 15.8 in textbook.
Explore photos of planetary nebulae and supernovae:
Planetary Nebulae: *https://hubblesite.org/images/gallery/34-planetary-nebulas*
Supernovae: *https://hubblesite.org/images/gallery/35-supernova-remnants*

Activity #7
Complete after reading 16.2 in textbook.
Determine which planets are visible in your night sky, and locate as many of them as you can.

Activity #8
Complete after reading 17.3 in textbook.
Explore photos of molecular clouds: *https://hubblesite.org/images/gallery/33-emission-nebulas*

Activity #9
Complete after reading 17.4 in textbook.
Learn more about the Hubble Deep Field Image and explore the methods astronomers use to number and classify the galaxies in the image: *http://deepfield.amazingspace.org/* ("The Hubble Deep Field Academy" by Amazing Space).

Chapter 13

Distances and Appearances

Mark "T" if the statement is true; mark "F" if the statement is false.

1. .... Nine light-years is the same as 54 trillion miles.

2. .... An AU is a greater distance than a light-year.

3. .... The Earth is one light-year from the Sun.

4. .... The closest star to the Sun is about four light-years away.

5. .... A light-year is a unit of time.

6. .... The two main units of distance in astronomy are the foot and the millimeter.

7. .... Jupiter is five AUs from the Sun, which is the same as 63,000 miles.

Circle the correct answer.

8. To us on Earth, Spica and Aldebaran appear to have the same brightness. In reality, Spica is 66 times brighter than Aldebaran. Spica must be much [closer to / farther from] the Earth than Aldebaran is.

9. Betelgeuse and Antares have exactly the same brightness in reality, but Betelgeuse appears to be brighter. This means that Betelgeuse is [closer to / farther from] the Earth than Antares is.

Star Charts: http://www.skymaps.com/downloads.html
http://www.midnightkite.com
Star Wheel: http://www.skyandtelescope.com/observing/make-a-star-wheel/

What Is True?

Mark "T" if the statement is true; mark "F" if the statement is false.

1. .... If you go star-gazing at 5 AM, you will not see all the same stars that you would see at 8 PM on the same day.

2. .... Polaris is one of the brightest stars in the sky.

3. .... Polaris is another name for the North Star.

4. .... Polaris is part of the constellation called Ursa Major.

Rotation and Revolution

Complete the sentences.

1. To .... means to travel in a circle around something else.

2. Polaris is the star directly above the North ....

3. At the .... the stars seem to move straight across the sky.

4. .... and Dubhe can be used to find the location of Polaris.

5. One .... of the Earth is the same as one day and one night.

Chapter 13

6. Polaris is a star in the Little Bear, a constellation that is called .... in Latin.

   _ _ _ _ _ (_) _ _

7. When you see Polaris in front of you, you know you are facing ....

   (_) _ _ _ _

8. The .... makes a wide circle around Polaris.

   _ _(_)_ _ _ _ _ _ _

9. .... and the Big Dipper are always on opposite sides of Polaris.

   _(_)_ _ _ _ _ _ _

10. An .... is the imaginary center line around which an object rotates.

    _(_)_ _

11. At the North Pole, the stars seem to travel around the sky in a ....

    _(_)_ _ _ _

12. .... is not a very bright star, but it is very important because it never moves all night long.

    _ _ _ _ _ _(_)

Fill in the Blank

Now use the circled letters above to fill in the right answers below!

The stars seem to move across the sky at night because the Earth is

_ _ _ _ _ _ _ _ on its _ _ _ _ .

76

Chapter 13

Chapter 13 Review

Answer in complete sentences.

1. What is astronomy?

2. What is a constellation?

3. What is a light-year?

4. What is an AU?

5. What does it mean to rotate?

6. What does it mean to revolve?

7. Why is Polaris special?

8. Why do we see different parts of the sky all night long?

   ....
   ....
   ....

9. Why do we see different stars at different times of the year?

   ....
   ....
   ....

10. How many degrees is a fist-width and a finger-width? What is latitude?

    ....
    ....
    ....
    ....

11. As Huckleberry Finn falls asleep on his raft on the Mississippi River, he notices that Merak and Dubhe are in the 9 o'clock position. When he wakes up, Merak and Dubhe are exactly between the 8 o'clock position and the 7 o'clock position. How long has Huck Finn been asleep?

    ....
    ....

Star-Gazing Test

Demonstrate that you can find the following constellations and stars in the sky without referring to a star chart.

Constellations: Orion, Canis Major, Canis Minor, Taurus, the Pleiades, Ursa Minor (the Little Dipper), the Big Dipper, and Cassiopeia

Stars: Betelgeuse, Sirius, Procyon, Polaris, Merak, and Dubhe

Chapter 14

Gravity and Orbits

Mark "T" if the statement is true; mark "F" if the statement is false.

1. .... Astronauts on the International Space Station feel completely weightless because there is no gravity in outer space.

2. .... An orbit is the path of an object around a planet or star.

3. .... A spacecraft in orbit is in a state of continuous freefall.

4. .... Our solar system is a collection of planets, asteroids, comets, and other objects orbiting the Sun.

5. .... The Sun is at the center of the solar system because it is the most massive object in the solar system.

6. .... Astronauts feel weightless because they are falling around the Earth.

7. .... The Earth exerts a gravitational pull on this workbook.

8. .... This workbook exerts a gravitational pull on the Earth.

9. .... The more massive an object is, the weaker its gravitational pull is.

10. .... The Earth stays in its orbit around the Sun because it is attached to a long string.

11. .... Balls, paper airplanes, and children fall towards the ground for the same reason that the ISS and the Moon orbit the Earth.

12. .... Bill Shepherd was commander of Expedition 1 on the International Space Station, and spent 138 consecutive days on the ISS. This means that he spent 138 days in freefall around the Earth.

CHECK IT OUT!

International Space Station:
https://www.nasa.gov/mission_pages/station/main/suni_iss_tour.html
https://www.nasa.gov/mission_pages/station/main/index.html
https://spotthestation.nasa.gov/sightings/
https://eol.jsc.nasa.gov/
Phases of the Moon: https://sepuplhs.org/middle/third-edition/simulations/moon_phase_simulation.html
Lunar eclipse animation: https://micro.magnet.fsu.edu/primer/java/scienceopticsu/lunar/index.html
Solar eclipse animation: https://micro.magnet.fsu.edu/primer/java/scienceopticsu/solar/index.html
NASA, lunar eclipses: https://eclipse.gsfc.nasa.gov/lunar.html
NASA, solar eclipses: https://eclipse.gsfc.nasa.gov/solar.html
Eclipse viewer: http://hilaroad.com/camp/projects/eclipse_viewer/eclipse_viewer.html
Tides: http://y2u.be/3RdkXs8BibE

Lunar Phases

Complete the sentences.

1. As the Moon .... the Earth, the side of the Moon that faces away from the Sun is always in darkness.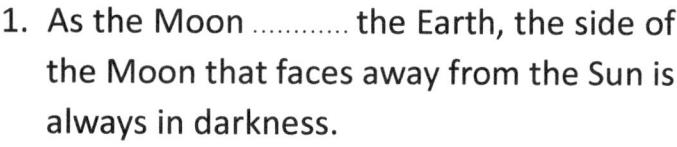

2. A .... moon is the phase in which we see only a sliver of the Moon.

3. A last quarter moon is the phase that occurs right after the waning .... moon.

4. Because the Moon is so large, its gravitational pull is strong enough to stabilize the .... of the Earth's axis.

5. The Earth has a very large moon compared with most .... of its size.

6. When we see more and more of the Moon each night, we say that the Moon is ....

7. A .... is the phase in which we see the Moon as a full circle.

8. When we see less and less of the Moon each night, we say that the Moon is ....

Fill in the Blank

Now use the circled letters above to fill in the right answer below!

The fact that the Moon is _ _ _ _ _ _ _ _ the Earth explains why the Moon has phases.

80 Chapter 14

More Lunar Phases

When the Sun, Moon, and Earth are aligned as shown below, what does the Moon look like from the Earth? Draw the visible part of the Moon and label it as a full moon, waning gibbous moon, last quarter moon, or waxing crescent moon. The first diagram is done for you.

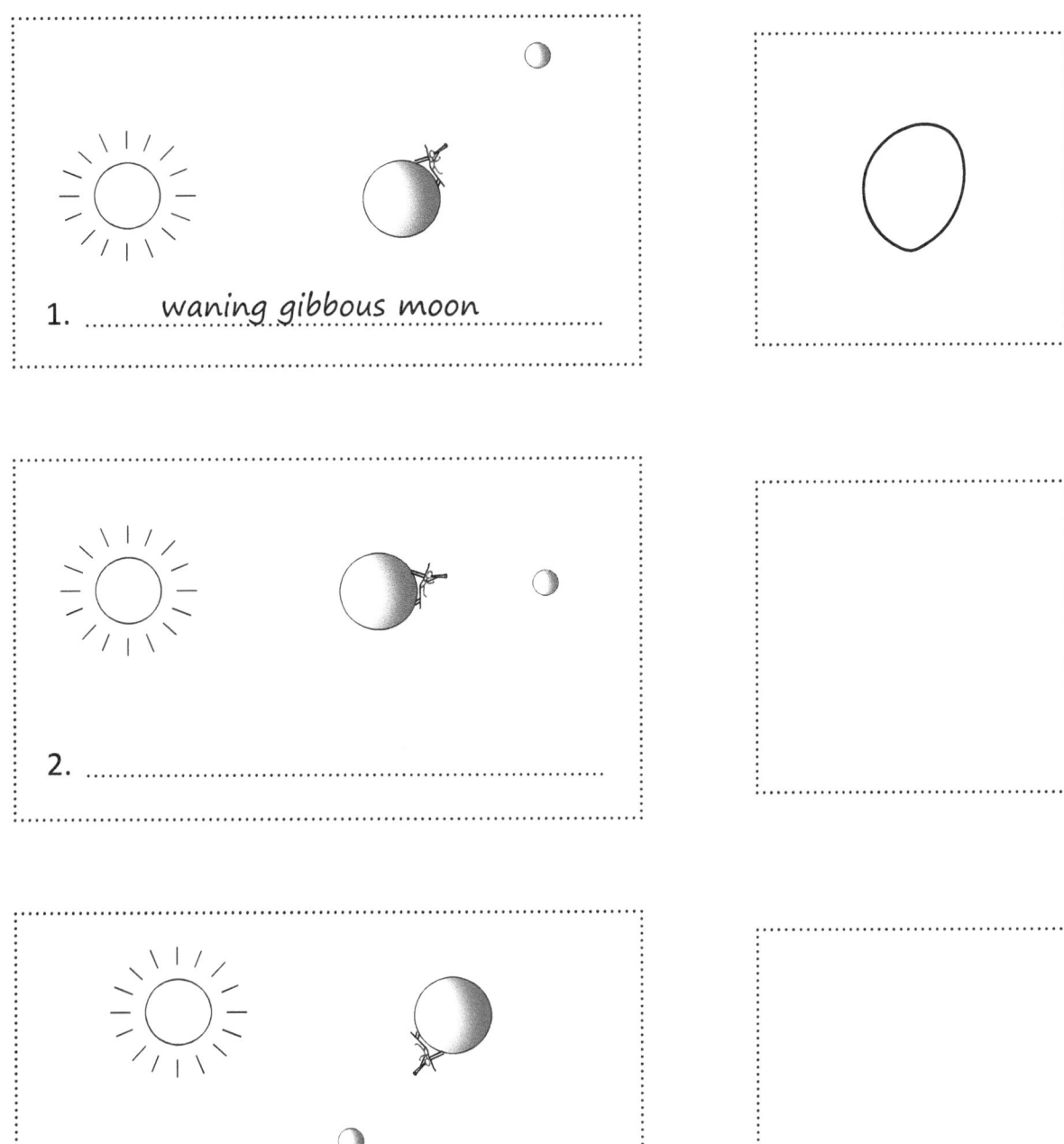

1. waning gibbous moon

2. ....

3. ....

Chapter 14

Lunar Eclipses

Match the diagrams to the photos by writing the name of the correct eclipse above each of the diagrams.

1. ....

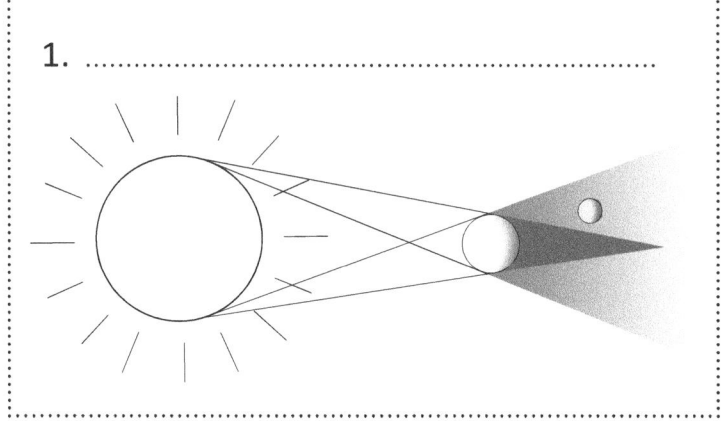

2. ....

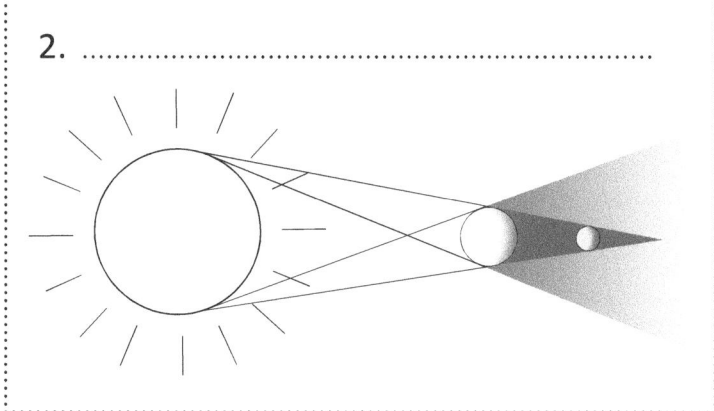

3. ....

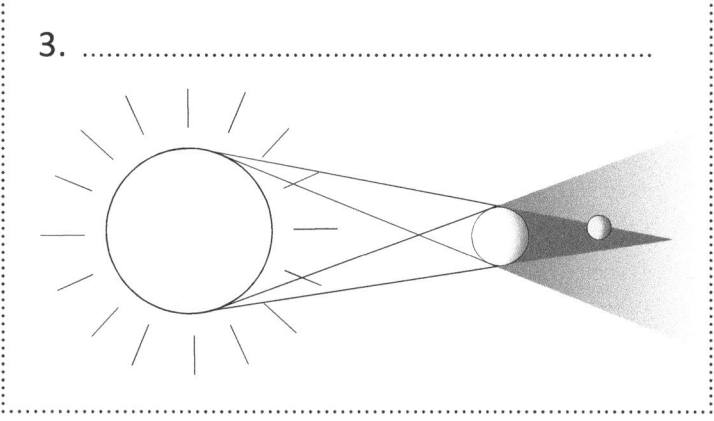

More Eclipses

Fill in the blanks to complete the sentences.

1. A lunar eclipse occurs when the .... shadow falls upon the

   ....

2. A solar eclipse occurs when the .... shadow falls upon the

   ....

3. During the period of totality, a radiant halo called the ....

   appears around the Sun.

4. *Circle the correct answer:* A partial solar eclipse occurs where the Moon's
   [umbra / penumbra] falls on the Earth.

5. Annular solar eclipses occur when the Moon is .... miles from
   the Earth.

6. Solar eclipses do not occur at every new moon because the Moon's orbit is slightly

   ....

7. Except during the few minutes of .... , it is not safe to view a
   solar eclipse with your naked eyes.

8. *Circle the correct answer:* To see a total solar eclipse, you have to be within the
   Moon's [umbra / penumbra].

Chapter 14 Review

Answer in complete sentences.

1. What does it mean to orbit?

   ....
   ....

2. Why have the Earth's seasons remained the same for thousands of years?

   ....
   ....
   ....

3. What are the phases of the Moon?

   ....
   ....

4. What is the penumbra of a shadow?

   ....
   ....

5. What is the umbra of a shadow?

   ....
   ....

6. When does a total lunar eclipse occur?

   ....
   ....

7. What are the three kinds of lunar eclipses?

   ....
   ....

8. What are the three kinds of solar eclipses?

   ....

   ....

9. *Circle all that apply:* The strength of gravity between two objects depends on ....

   a. their color   b. their distance from each other

   c. whether they are made of magnetic materials   d. their mass

10. *Circle the correct answer:* The force of gravity is [*strongest / weakest*] when you are nearby and [*strongest / weakest*] when you are far away.

11. What happens when gravity pulls on something that is very large?

    ....

    ....

Label the umbra and penumbra in the following diagrams.

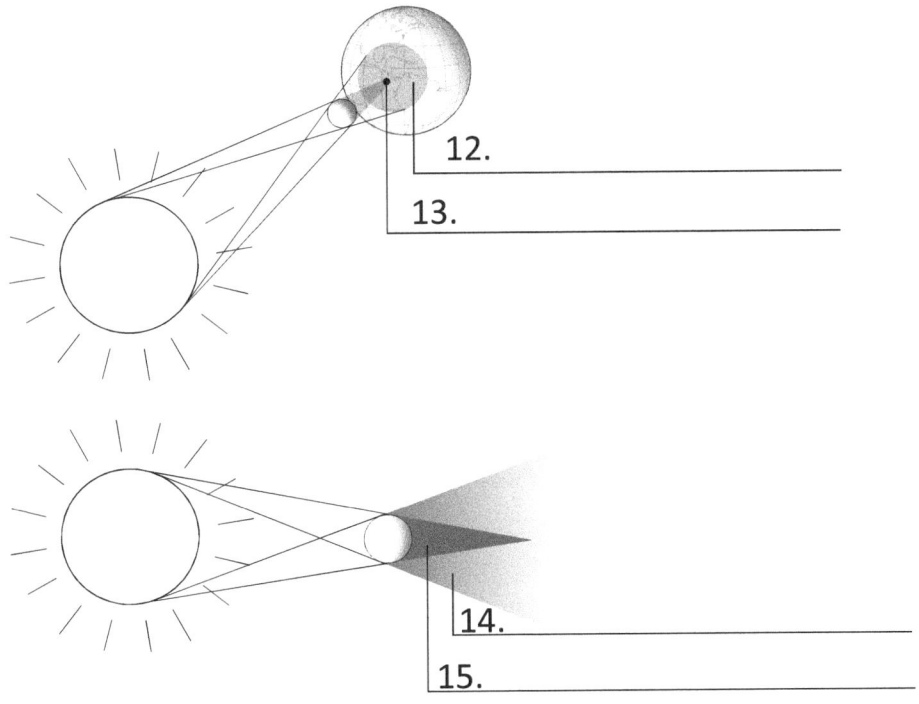

12. _____

13. _____

14. _____

15. _____

Chapter 14   85

Chapter 15

What Is True?

Mark "T" if the statement is true; mark "F" if the statement is false.

1. .... The Earth is surrounded by a giant magnetic field because it is a huge magnet.

2. .... Without an atmosphere, the entire Earth would be a lush, tropical paradise.

3. .... Aurorae are caused by the interaction of the solar wind with the Earth's gravity.

4. .... Each second, approximately one million tons of particles escape from the Sun in the solar wind.

5. .... The pull of the Earth's gravity is the same as the pull of the Earth's magnetism.

6. .... The arrow of a magnetic compass turns to point north because it is lining itself up with the Earth's magnetic field.

7. .... If it weren't for the Earth's magnetic field, the solar wind would have stripped away the Earth's atmosphere a long time ago.

8. .... The solar wind consists of energetic, "speedy" particles that escape the pull of the Sun's gravity and shoot into outer space.

9. .... The Earth's magnetic field is produced by the motions of the molten copper in the Earth's outer core.

10. .... Aurorae occur when some of the particles in the solar wind manage to penetrate the Earth's magnetic field.

11. .... The magnetic field acts as a magnetic shield that changes the particles in the solar wind into meteors, or shooting stars.

12. .... When particles of the solar wind enter the Earth's atmosphere, they collide with atoms of hydrogen and carbon dioxide.

Space weather: https://www.exploratorium.edu/spaceweather/index.html
Aurora Live Cam: https://explore.org/livecams/zen-den/northern-lights-cam

Fill in the Blanks

Fill in the blanks to complete the sentences.

1. The Sun's enormous .... allows it to produce its own energy.

2. The Sun is about .... miles in diameter and has .... times as much mass as the Earth.

3. The Sun is a gigantic ball of .... and helium gases.

4. The surface of the Sun is ....°F, and the Sun's core is ....°F.

5. Gravity is a force that acts on ...., and the more .... an object has, the stronger its gravity is.

6. The Sun's .... is the reason why the gases in the Sun do not turn into wisps of cloud and float away.

7. The gases in the Sun are held together in the shape of a ball by their own ....

8. The Sun shines by its own energy, but all the other objects in the solar system shine because they are .... the light of the Sun.

9. The Sun's incredible mass turns it into an enormous furnace that produces light and heat through ....

Chapter 15

Nuclear Fusion

Mark "T" if the statement is true; mark "F" if the statement is false.

1. .... The Sun's core is made out of a gas.

2. .... When two nuclei slam into each other at tremendous speeds, they can combine to form a smaller, lighter nucleus.

3. .... A cupful of the material in the Sun's core would weigh about 50 pounds on Earth.

4. .... Nuclear fusion releases energy in the form of an infrared ray.

5. .... The Sun's gravity is so strong that the Sun's inner core is crushed by the weight of the Sun's outer layers.

6. .... The Sun's gravity is incredibly strong because of the Sun's bright color.

7. .... Temperature is our way of measuring how much energy is possessed by the individual particles in an object.

8. .... When an object is very hot, its particles move very slowly.

9. .... Nuclear fusion is possible in the Sun's hydrogen core because the hydrogen is so hot that it is moving at incredibly fast speeds.

10. .... When five hydrogen nuclei slam into each other in just the right order, the result is a helium nucleus.

11. .... All the light and heat that we receive from the Sun started out as gamma rays released by colliding hydrogen nuclei.

Gamma Rays to Sunshine

Mark "T" if the statement is true; mark "F" if the statement is false.

1. .... If four hydrogen nuclei fused into a helium nucleus on Earth, the energy released would destroy everything around for at least two miles.

2. .... Gamma rays carry much more energy than do rays of ordinary sunshine.

3. .... A single gamma ray does not carry very much energy.

4. .... Electromagnetic radiation is a way of transferring mass through electromagnetic waves.

5. .... The Sun generates so many gamma rays that a single second's worth would be enough to meet the entire world's energy needs for the next 500,000 years.

6. .... Gamma rays travel at the speed of light, so after they are released by nuclear fusion, they reach the Earth almost instantly.

7. .... It takes a gamma ray hundreds of thousands of years just to travel from the core to the surface of the Sun.

8. .... Gamma rays have to zigzag all through the core of the Sun before they can escape to the surface. This is because the Sun is so dense.

9. .... It would be a good thing if the Sun's energy reached us as gamma rays instead of as visible light.

10. .... After zigzagging through the Sun for hundreds of thousands of years, a gamma ray emerges just as energetic and powerful as ever.

11. .... Visible light carries just the right amount of energy to power the process of photosynthesis in plants.

Chapter 15

Low-Mass Stars

Fill in the blanks to complete the sentences.

1. A low-mass star ends its life as a .... star surrounded by a ....

2. Scientists say that a star has died when the process of .... ends in the star's core.

3. Some stars shine for as long as one trillion years, but all stars eventually run out of ....

4. When nuclear fusion in a star stops, the amount of energy in the core ....

5. After nuclear fusion stops, the core of the star is no longer full of energetic .... , and gravity is able to compress the helium core even more.

6. The helium in the star's core becomes denser and hotter as it is compressed by the force of ....

7. When the star's helium core reaches a temperature of 180,000,000°F, helium begins to be fused into ....

8. It takes higher .... to fuse helium than it takes to fuse hydrogen.

9. The factor that determines how a star ends its life is its .... , because the strength of a star's gravity depends on its mass.

10. The carbon core of a .... star never gets hot enough to fuse into anything else, because the star's gravity is not strong enough to compress the core any farther.

11. The outer layers of a low-mass star drift away in gigantic clouds of gas, called a ....

12. A white dwarf star is a glowing ball of hot, dense ....

13. A cupful of white-dwarf material on Earth would weigh the same as twelve ....

14. Pencil lead and diamonds are both made out of carbon—the only difference is that diamonds are much, much .... than pencil lead.

15. A white dwarf eventually cools so much that it no longer gives off light. Then it is called a .... dwarf star.

16. Even though nuclear fusion is not occurring in its core, a white dwarf star is called a star because its .... makes it shine.

Science Notebook

Illustrate hydrogen fusion in your Science Notebook, referring to Figure 15.9 in the textbook.

High-Mass Stars and Supernovae

Mark "T" if the statement is true; mark "F" if the statement is false.

1. .... Iron can't be fused like hydrogen, helium, carbon, neon, oxygen, and silicon.

2. .... A supernova explosion can outshine an entire galaxy.

3. .... A supernova occurs when the iron core of a high-mass star fuses into platinum.

4. .... Supernova remnants can only be seen for a few years after the supernova itself.

5. .... The gold in your parents' wedding rings was fused in a supernova.

Write "High-mass stars," "Low-mass stars," or "All stars" to fill in the blanks below.

6. .... are at least eight times as massive as the Sun.

7. .... end up as supernova explosions.

8. .... end up as white dwarf stars and planetary nebulae.

9. In ...., nuclear fusion stops when the fuel runs out.

10. .... do not have enough gravity to compress their carbon cores.

11. In ...., carbon is fused into neon or oxygen.

12. In ...., hydrogen is fused into helium.

13. .... reach temperatures of nine billion degrees.

14. .... will eventually run out of fuel.

Science Notebook

Illustrate helium fusion in your Science Notebook, referring to Figure 15.12 in the textbook.

Chapter 15 Review

Answer in complete sentences.

1. What is an aurora?

2. What is the solar wind?

3. What is nuclear fusion?

4. What are gamma rays?

5. What is a planetary nebula?

6. What is a white dwarf star?

7. What is a supernova?

Fill in the blanks to complete the diagram. Then draw and label the diagram in your Science Notebook.

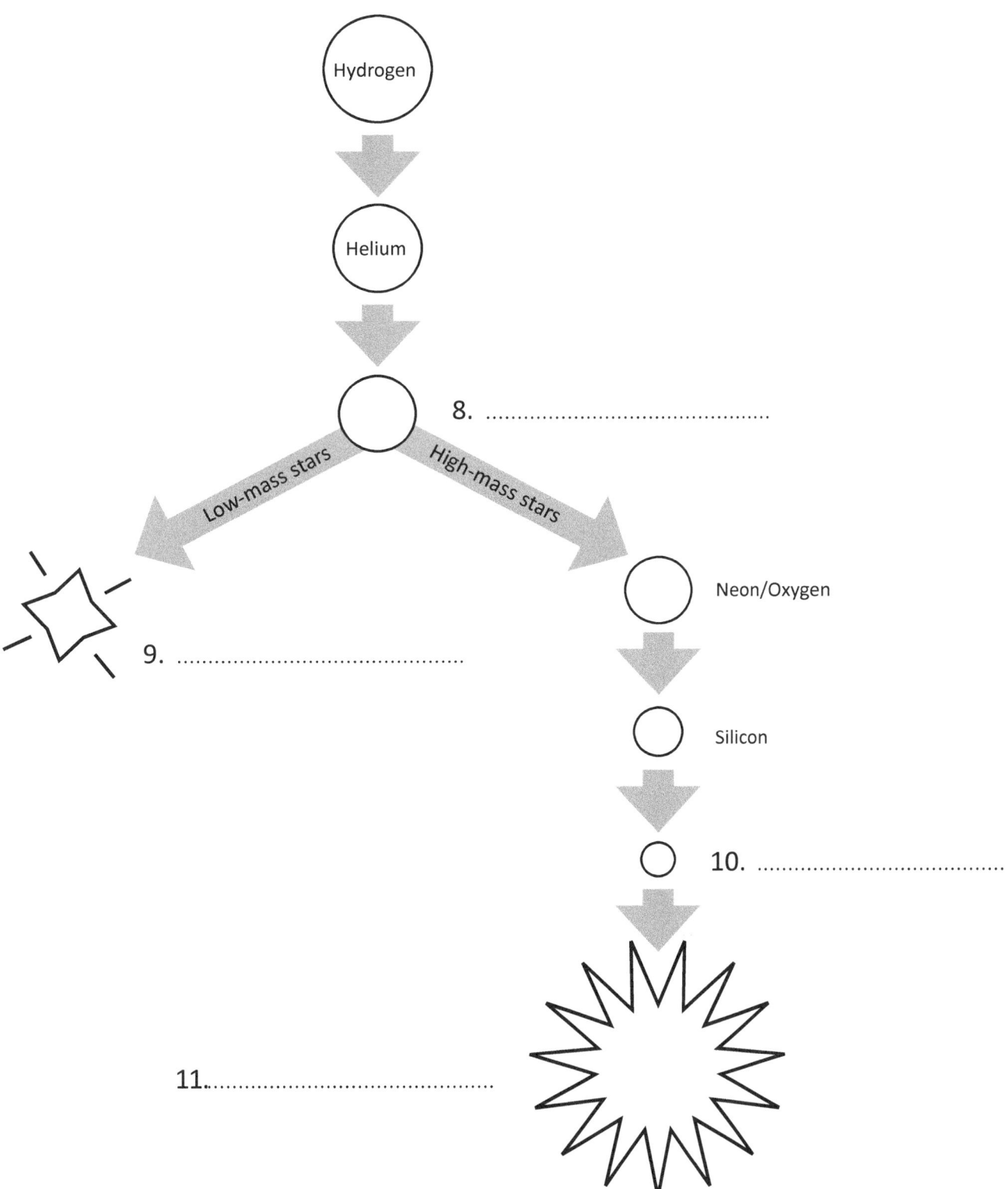

8. ....

9. ....

10. ....

11. ....

Chapter 15

Chapter 16

Terrestrial or Jovian?

Mark "T" if the statement is true; mark "F" if the statement is false.

1. .... The word "planet" means "pioneer" in Greek.

2. .... The planets never travel more than one fist above or below the Sun's path through the sky.

3. .... The five naked-eye planets are Mercury, Venus, Neptune, Jupiter, and Uranus.

4. .... When Venus appears in the evening, it is known as the Evening Star; when Venus appears in the morning, it is known as the Morning Star.

5. .... The terrestrial planets are also called gas giants.

6. .... The jovian planets do not have solid surfaces.

7. .... Mercury, Venus, Earth, and Mars are made of rocks and metals.

8. .... Jupiter, Saturn, Uranus, and Neptune are balls of hydrogen and helium.

9. .... Jupiter is closer to the Sun than Neptune is.

10. .... Venus is farther from the Sun than the Earth is.

11. .... Saturn is closer to the Earth than Uranus is.

12. .... The planets revolve around the Sun and rotate on their axes.

CHECK IT OUT!

Size of the solar system: https://theskylive.com/3dsolarsystem
Weight on different planets: https://www.exploratorium.edu/ronh/weight/index.html
https://www.schoolsobservatory.org/discover/sims-cals/gravsim
Sky at a Glance: https://www.skyandtelescope.com/observing/sky-at-a-glance/

Greenhouse Effect

Complete the sentences.

1. Because Mercury has such weak .... , any gases that originally covered Mercury would tend to drift away into space.

2. One reason for the planet's extreme temperatures is that Mercury .... very slowly on its axis.

3. The Earth's molten iron core becomes a .... when it is "sloshed around" as the Earth rotates.

4. Since Mercury lacks an atmosphere, infrared radiation from the warm soil escapes into .... at night, leaving the night-time side of Mercury freezing cold.

5. Mercury's loss of its .... was mainly due to the solar wind.

6. The greenhouse effect can be seen on a smaller scale in .... and parked cars.

Chapter 16

7. Everything that is warm .... thermal energy through infrared radiation.

    _ _ _ _ _ _(_)_

8. Carbon dioxide and .... are examples of greenhouse gases.

    _ _ _ _   _ _ _ _(_)

9. Greenhouse gases allow rays of sunshine to pass through, but block the passage of .... radiation.

    _ _ _ _ _ _(_)_

Fill in the Blank

Now use the circled letters above to fill in the right answer below!

> Mercury has such extreme temperatures because it lacks an
>
> _ _ _ _ _ _ _ _ _ _ .

Science Notebook

Illustrate the greenhouse effect in your Science Notebook, referring to Figure 16.4 or Figure 16.5 in the textbook.

Jupiter and the Asteroid Belt

Fill in the blanks to complete the sentences.

1. There is a gap of almost .... AU's between Mars and Jupiter.

2. The .... contains most of the asteroids in the solar system.

3. Asteroids are large chunks of rock and metal that .... the Sun.

4. Asteroids have very irregular shapes because they are much less .... than planets.

5. The largest asteroid in the asteroid belt is named ....

6. On average, the asteroids in the asteroid belt are .... of miles apart.

7. .... acts as a giant "sweeper" to clear away asteroids from the inner solar system.

8. Even the .... wobbles a little because of the strength of Jupiter's gravitational pull.

9. Some asteroids collided with Jupiter. Others were flung to the outermost regions of the ....

10. Jupiter .... extremely quickly.

11. Jupiter is orbited by over sixty ....

Chapter 16

12. .... is the largest moon in the solar system.

13. Jupiter's Galilean moons are made of ...., ..., and ....

14. Callisto, Ganymede, and .... may have deep oceans of liquid water beneath their icy surfaces.

15. Io is the most volcanically active place in the solar system because it is being stretched and pulled in different directions by the strength of Jupiter's ....

Virtual Tour of the Solar System: https://www.solarsystemscope.com/
https://trek.nasa.gov/
Scale model of solar system: https://www.exploratorium.edu/ronh/solar_system/index.html
https://www.noao.edu/education/peppercorn/pcmain.html

Planet Facts

Fill in the blanks to complete the sentences.

1. .... is the smallest of the eight planets.

2. .... has the most impressive ring system in the solar system.

3. .... is exactly 1 AU from the Sun.

4. The atmosphere of .... is so dense, it is almost like a liquid.

5. .... is the brightest object in the sky besides the Sun and Moon.

6. .... is the largest planet in the solar system.

7. The Great Red Spot is a huge storm on ....

8. Like Uranus, ... has a blue-green color.

9. Someone who weighs 100 pounds on Earth would weigh 107 pounds on ....

10. .... is the farthest planet from the Sun.

11. .... is covered with large oceans and flowing rivers.

12. .... is the smallest gas giant.

13. Olympus Mons, one of the tallest mountains in the solar system, is found on ....

Chapter 16

14. Besides the Earth, ... is the only terrestrial planet that contains a significant amount of water.

15. .... travels along its orbit like a rolling ball, because its axis is tilted by 98°.

16. .... is almost the same size as the Earth.

17. If .... were 80 times more massive, it would be a small star.

18. .... is the planet closest to the Sun.

Science Notebook

*Research the Vatican Observatory **or** Halley's Comet and write a brief report in your Science Notebook. Share your findings with your family!*

Chapter 16 Review

Answer in complete sentences.

1. List the five planets (besides Earth!) that can be seen without a telescope.

   ....
   ....
   ....
   ....
   ....

2. What are the main features of the terrestrial planets?

   ....
   ....
   ....

3. What are the main features of the jovian planets?

   ....
   ....
   ....
   ....

4. What is the greenhouse effect?

   ....
   ....
   ....
   ....

5. What is atmospheric pressure?

   ....
   ....
   ....

6. Why would you weigh more on Jupiter than on Earth?

   ....
   ....
   ....
   ....

7. What is the Kuiper Belt?

   ....
   ....
   ....

8. What are comets?

   ....
   ....
   ....

9. When do comets grow tails?

   ....
   ....

10. What are meteors?

    ....
    ....
    ....

Mark "T" if the statement is true; mark "F" if the statement is false.

11. .... Venus is larger than Saturn.

12. .... Mars looks red because of its methane atmosphere.

13. .... Pluto is a dwarf planet.

14. .... Mars experiences four seasons just as the Earth does.

15. .... Jupiter is orbited by two moons, called Phobos and Deimos.

16. .... Saturn's moon, Titan, is one of the largest moons in the solar system.

17. .... Mercury has extreme temperatures because of its thick atmosphere.

18. .... The polar ice caps on Mars are made of frozen carbon dioxide and water.

19. .... Jovian planets rotate extremely quickly.

20. .... Ganymede, Callisto, Io, and Europa are dwarf planets in the Kuiper Belt.

21. .... Meteors glow because of the friction between them and the air.

Chapter 17

Galaxies and More

Mark "T" if the statement is true; mark "F" if the statement is false.

1. .... The Milky Way is actually made of milk.
2. .... The Milky Way is about 100,000 light-years across, which is the distance that light can travel in 10 minutes.
3. .... The average distance between the stars in our part of the Milky Way is about five light-years, which is the same as three miles to a grain of sand.
4. .... In the Milky Way, everything revolves around the bulge in the center of the galaxy.
5. .... The Milky Way is so huge that it takes about 100 million years for a star to make a complete circle and return to where it started.
6. .... All galaxies have the same shape.
7. .... A spiral galaxy is shaped like a flying saucer with a thick center and long, pinwheel arms.
8. .... The Sun is located in the Scutum-Centaurus Arm of the Milky Way.
9. .... If the solar system were moved to the galactic bulge, it would never be dark at night.
10. .... There are more supernovae on the edges of the Milky Way than there are in the galactic bulge.
11. .... All the copper, nitrogen, and sodium on Earth were fused in the high temperatures of long-past supernovae.
12. .... If a supernova occurred near the solar system, we would only hear a small "pop," if we even noticed the event at all.

Size of the universe:
http://y2u.be/bhofN1xX6u0
https://micro.magnet.fsu.edu/primer/java/scienceopticsu/powersof10/

Birth of Stars

Fill in the blanks to complete the sentences.

1. When a star dies, it releases much of its matter in either a planetary nebula or a ....

2. The matter released by a dying star becomes part of a .... cloud, and is formed into a new ....

3. Some of the gas and .... in molecular clouds has been around since the beginning of the galaxy.

4. A molecular cloud starts to condense when it is nudged by .... from supernovae.

5. As the dust and gas in a molecular cloud move together, their gravity becomes ....

6. After several .... years of being compressed by its own gravity, the center of a globule is as dense as the inside of Jupiter.

7. Jupiter was not .... enough to become a star.

8. As a globule condenses, the gases in its inner regions become extremely dense and ....

9. Eventually, the crushing gravity produces such high temperatures in the globule's core that .... begins.

10. The eight planets, the asteroids, the comets, and the moons were formed from gas and dust on the outer edges of the ....

11. The planets orbit around the Sun because they were formed from a globule that started .... around its center as it condensed.

Chapter 17

What Is True?

Mark "T" if the statement is true; mark "F" if the statement is false.

1. _____ The Milky Way is the entire universe.

2. _____ Scientists estimate that there are 1500 galaxies in the part of the universe that they can see from Earth.

3. _____ Each galaxy is located about a hundred miles from every other galaxy.

4. _____ The galaxies are not sprinkled at random across the sky.

5. _____ The Milky Way and the Andromeda Galaxy are the largest galaxies in the Local Group (see Figure 17.9).

6. _____ The Local Group contains about 10 million galaxies, most of them smaller than the Milky Way.

7. _____ The Local Group is part of a much larger structure called the Virgo Supercluster.

8. _____ The Eridanus Cluster is part of the Virgo Supercluster (see Figure 17.10).

9. _____ The Virgo Supercluster is rather small compared to other superclusters.

10. _____ The Centaurus Supercluster is located near the Virgo Supercluster (see Figure 17.11).

11. _____ The Ophiuchus Supercluster is located below the Virgo Supercluster (see Figure 17.11).

12. _____ The Capricornus Void is located next to the Ursa Major Supercluster (see Figure 17.11).

13. _____ Superclusters are the largest patterns in the universe.

14. _____ A void is an empty space.

15. _____ God created the universe to be our home.

The Big Bang Theory

Fill in the blanks to complete the sentences.

1. The Big Bang theory explains what the universe was probably like right after ....

2. According to the Big Bang theory, the universe began as a huge explosion, which was the beginning of .... and ....

3. In scientific language, "......................................" means a hypothesis, or guess, that has been confirmed by experiments.

4. When the universe was first expanding, it consisted of an extremely hot "soup" of tiny .... of matter and energy.

5. The protons, neutrons, and electrons in the early universe were too hot and energetic to "stick together" as ....

6. As the universe expanded and became less dense, it also became ....

7. It took the universe about a .... years to expand and cool enough for stars and galaxies to form.

8. Much of the gas in molecular clouds is a remnant of the .... and .... clouds in the early universe.

Chapter 17

9. Scientists currently estimate that the universe is .... billion years old.

10. Scientists estimate the .... of the universe by calculating how long it must have taken the universe to expand to its current state.

11. The .... in the universe are moving away from each other at tremendous speeds.

12. The gravitational pull of each galaxy holds all its .... together in a single group.

13. .... , a famous astronomer, provided definite proof that the universe is expanding.

14. .... , a Catholic priest and a brilliant physicist, proposed the Big Bang theory as an explanation for the expansion of the universe.

15. The name ".. ...." is actually a phrase that one scientist used to make fun of Lemaitre's theory.

16. Probably the main reason Lemaitre's theory was so unpopular is that most of the scientists of his time believed the world was eternal and self-.. .

17. *Circle the correct answer:* The Big Bang theory [*does / does not*] prove that God did not create the universe.

18. Our little planet Earth simply could never have existed if the universe weren't just the .... it is.

19. If the universe were less ....—that is, if it had less "stuff" in it—the Big Bang would have blown all the protons and atoms apart so quickly that there would be no time for galaxies, stars, and planets to form.

20. If the universe were more massive—that is, heavier, with more "stuff" in it—the Big Bang would not have been powerful enough to make it ....

21. Stars that are larger than the Sun have so much mass that they are .... and often ....

22. If the solar system were in a smaller galaxy, there might not have been enough .... to produce the elements needed for life on Earth.

Hubble images: https://hubblesite.org
https://spaceplace.nasa.gov/
https://www.dvidshub.net/unit/NASA
Astronomy Picture of the Day: https://apod.nasa.gov/apod/

Chapter 17

Chapter 17 Review

Answer in complete sentences.

1. What is a galaxy?

   ....
   ....
   ....

2. How many stars are there in the Milky Way?

   ....
   ....
   ....

3. What are spiral galaxies?

   ....
   ....
   ....

4. What are molecular clouds?

   ....
   ....
   ....

5. What are globules?

   ....
   ....
   ....

6. What does the Big Bang theory say about the beginning of the universe?

   ....

   ....

   ....

7. What is a singularity?

   ....

   ....

   ....

8. How exact did the Big Bang explosion have to be?

   ....

   ....

   ....

9. What would have happened if the universe were less massive at the time of the Big Bang?

   ....

   ....

   ....

Science Notebook

In your Science Notebook, copy down the quotations from Church teaching on pgs. 348-349 in your textbook.

Unit 3 Test

Multiple choice: Circle the correct answer.

1. Betelgeuse is a star in which constellation?

    a. Taurus   b. Orion   c. Ursa Major

2. Because of the Earth's rotation on its axis, the stars appear to circle around

    a. Polaris   b. Betelgeuse   c. Sirius   d. the Moon

3. *Circle the answer that is **not** true:* Gravity is the reason that

    a. we have high and low tides   b. the solar wind does not strip away Earth's atmosphere
    c. the ISS orbits the Earth   d. molecular clouds contract into stars
    e. apples fall to the ground   f. the inside of the Sun is so dense

4. A solar eclipse occurs when

    a. the Sun passes between the Earth and the Moon
    b. the Moon passes between the Sun and the Earth
    c. the Earth passes between the Sun and the Moon

5. Earth's magnetic field protects Earth's atmosphere from

    a. aliens   b. the solar wind   c. electromagnetic radiation   d. asteroids

6. When four hydrogen nuclei fuse into a helium nucleus, they release energy in the form of

    a. a huge explosion   b. two gamma rays
    c. three rays of visible light   d. infrared light

7. A low-mass star will end its life as

   a. a supernova   b. a planet   c. a white dwarf star

8. *Circle the answer that is **not** true:* Supernovae

   a. create new elements
   b. distribute elements throughout the galaxy
   c. occur when a low-mass star dies
   d. are powerful enough to destroy life on Earth

9. Jovian planets

   a. do not have solid surfaces   b. are made mostly of rocks and metals
   c. do not have moons

10. The tail of a comet always points

    a. towards the Sun   b. behind the comet
    c. away from the Sun   d. towards the Earth

11. A molecular cloud is a place where

    a. new stars are formed   b. supernovae become oblong galaxies
    c. gravity has no effect

12. According to the Big Bang theory

    a. God did not create the world
    b. the universe began as a tiny, dense singularity
    c. the clusters of galaxies are drawing closer together

13. The Big Bang theory was proposed by

    a. Albert Einstein   b. Galileo Galilei   c. Georges Lemaitre   d. Tycho Brahe

Experiments

Supply List

Experiment #1:
kitchen scale
1-cup measuring cup
1 cup rice
1 cup sugar
1 cup flour
1 cup rice crispies
1 cup rolled oats
1 cup brown sugar, packed
1 cup water
1 cup oil
1 cup peanut butter
1 cup molasses

Experiment #2:
tall glass of water
raw egg in shell
¼ cup salt

Experiment #3:
large glass jar or drinking glass
molasses
water
oil
various small objects (an eraser, a paper clip, a cork, a grape, grains of rice, a whole peanut, a dried bean, etc.)

Experiment #4:
1 cup of heavy whipping cream, room temperature
electric mixer
salt (optional)

Experiment #5:
1 cup hydrogen peroxide, 3% solution
2 tsp. active dry yeast
glass or plastic bottle (about the size of a water bottle)
uninflated balloon
rubber band

Experiment #6:
empty plastic water bottle

Experiment #7:
empty glass soda bottle
quarter

Experiment #8:
empty soda can
stove with exposed elements (not a glass-top stove)
tongs
bowl of cold water

Experiment #9:
ice cube tray
water
milk
oil
rubbing alcohol
salt water
soda pop or sugar water

Experiment #10:
plastic cup
water

Experiment #11:
½ cup water
1 cup flour
bowl

Experiment #12:
empty glass bottle with a cork (such as a wine bottle)
2 tablespoons baking soda
½ cup household vinegar

Experiment #13:
rice sock or hot-and-cold pack (*not electric*)
3 kitchen utensils—1 plastic, 1 wood, and 1 metal—of similar lengths and with handles of similar thicknesses
3 large plastic drinking cups of similar sizes
water

Experiment #14:
clear glass casserole dish
eyedropper or drinking straw
dye (milk can be used instead of dye)
3 coffee mugs of the same height
water

Experiment #15:
2 balloons
wool garment
empty plastic bottle (water bottle, soda bottle, etc.)
scotch tape

Experiment #16:
balloon
wool garment
unflavored gelatin
rolled oats

Experiment #17:
3 bar or horseshoe magnets (not refrigerator magnets) of similar strength
string
iron filings (You can collect iron filings by running a magnet through dry soil or sand.)

Experiment #18 (Optional):
fluorescent light tube
balloon
wool garment

Experiment #19:
large, raw potato, 2-3 inches in diameter
paring knife
string
small weight (such as a bag or bucket of coins)
wooden pencil with flat sides

Experiment #20:
string
2 large, raw potatoes
2 pencils with smooth sides
a small weight (such as a bag or bucket of coins)
sharp knife

Experiment #21:
stalk of celery

Experiment #22:
3-4 large, round kitchen bowls
aluminum foil
direct sunlight

Experiment #23:
packet of bean seeds
large container for planting (dish or potting tray)
small container (plastic cup, small pot, the bottom of an empty water bottle)
soil
water
shoebox (or a similar box)
brown cardboard (or another dark color—cardboard with a white finish will reflect the light)
tape
scissors
rubber band

Experiment #24:
paper towels
water
waxed paper
sunshine or a warm room

Experiment #25:
bucket
watering can or hose
water
1-2 shovelfuls of soil
cheesecloth, thin fabric, screen, or sieve
2 bean plants of the same size that look equally healthy, saved from Experiment #23

Experiment #26:
2 small bowls, of similar size and material
plastic wrap
water
direct sunlight

Experiments — Chapter 2

Experiment #1

Mass and Density

Supplies:
kitchen scale
1-cup measuring cup
1 cup rice
1 cup sugar
1 cup flour
1 cup rice crispies
1 cup rolled oats
1 cup brown sugar, packed
1 cup water
1 cup oil
1 cup peanut butter
1 cup molasses

Observation: Some things are denser than others.

Question: What are the relative densities of 10 household ingredients?

Hypothesis: Form a hypothesis, or guess, by predicting the relative densities of the 10 ingredients listed. List the ingredients in your Science Notebook in order of how dense you think each one is.

Method:

1. Measure out exactly one cup of rice. Place the measuring cup and the rice on the kitchen scale and record its weight. Return the rice to its container.

2. Repeat step 1 with all the other ingredients. Record the exact weight of each ingredient in your Science Notebook.

Note: It is important that you use the same measuring cup for each ingredient. You will need to rinse out the cup between each of the wet ingredients, so you may want to save these ingredients for last.

Interpretation and Conclusion:
Using the data you have recorded for each ingredient, list the ingredients in order of their actual densities. Compare the results of your experiment with the predictions of your hypothesis.

No kitchen scale? You can construct a makeshift one by attaching a plastic bag to a rubber band and hanging it from your finger. Instead of weighing the ingredients by placing them on a kitchen scale, place the measuring cup and each ingredient into the plastic bag. Use a ruler to measure how far the rubber band stretches for each ingredient. The rubber band will stretch farthest for the densest ingredients. Since your makeshift scale is not as precise as a real scale, you may want to weigh only flour, rice crispies, sugar, water, and molasses.

Experiments : : Chapter 2

Experiment #2

Floating Egg

Supplies:
tall glass of water
raw egg in shell
¼ cup salt

Place the egg in the glass of water. The egg will sink to the bottom. Remove the egg and stir ¼ cup of salt into the water. Stir until dissolved. Place the egg in the water again. The egg will float!

What just happened?
An egg is denser than fresh water, so it sinks to the bottom of the glass. When you add salt to the fresh water, the water becomes more dense until it eventually becomes denser than the egg. The buoyant force pushes the egg upward and the egg floats!

Experiment #3

Liquid Layers

Supplies:
large glass jar or drinking glass
molasses
water
oil
various small objects (an eraser, a paper clip, a cork, a grape, grains of rice, a whole peanut, a dried bean, etc.)

1. Pour molasses into the glass jar until it is about one inch deep. Carefully pour one or two inches of water on the top of the molasses. To keep the two liquids from mixing, hold a spoon just above the molasses and pour the water onto the spoon first, instead of directly onto the molasses.

2. Pour one or two inches of oil on top of the water, again using a spoon to keep the liquids from mixing. The oil should float on top of the water and the water should float on top of the molasses.

3. Gently drop several small objects into the jar of liquids. Which objects are most dense? Which are least dense? Record the results in your Science Notebook.

Note: If you wash the objects before floating them in the jar of molasses, oil, and water, you can reuse the molasses to make gingerbread, molasses cookies, or some other recipe. Just pour off the water and oil and use the molasses right away.

Experiment #4

Physical Separation

A mixture can be separated into its parts by physical processes. Cream is a mixture of water and tiny bits of fat. (Cream also contains a small amount of proteins and minerals.) When the cream is churned (mixed), the fat starts to clump together into balls of butter. The buttermilk that is left behind is mostly water. Note: Since we are not going to sour the cream before churning it, your buttermilk will be much less acidic than store-bought buttermilk.

Supplies:
1 cup of heavy whipping cream, room temperature
electric mixer
salt (optional)

1. The first step is to separate the butterfat from the buttermilk. Beat the cream for several minutes until it begins to clump into small balls of butterfat. As you continue to beat the cream, more and more buttermilk will be released. You can pour the buttermilk into a separate bowl every few minutes to minimize splashing.

2. When the clumps of butter join together into a single ball of butter, turn off the mixer and pour out the remaining buttermilk. Save the buttermilk to drink or to use in a recipe. Rinse the butter by pouring clean water on it and kneading it with a spoon until the water becomes cloudy. Pour off the water and rinse the butter again.

3. Your butter is now finished! If you want salted butter, you can sprinkle in up to ¼ tsp. of salt. Be sure to beat the butter thoroughly after adding the salt. Your homemade butter can be molded into a roll and wrapped in plastic wrap to store in the refrigerator.

Experiments : : Chapter 2

Experiment #5

Chemical Separation

Unlike mixtures, compounds can only be separated by chemical processes. In this experiment you will see how a chemical reaction can be used to separate hydrogen peroxide into water and oxygen.

Supplies:
1 cup hydrogen peroxide, 3% solution
2 tsp. active dry yeast
glass or plastic bottle (about the size of a water bottle)
uninflated balloon
rubber band

1. Pour 1 cup of hydrogen peroxide into the plastic bottle.

2. Measure two teaspoons of active dry yeast onto a tissue or piece of paper towel. Carefully fold the tissue around the yeast. If the mouth of your bottle is small, roll the tissue into a burrito-like package to fit it into the bottle.

3. Practice fitting the uninflated balloon over the mouth of the bottle. When you are ready, push the package of yeast into the bottle and quickly fit the balloon over the mouth of the bottle. Wrap the rubber band tightly around the bottle mouth to seal the balloon onto the bottle.

4. When the hydrogen peroxide soaks through the tissue, the mixture will begin to foam and expand rapidly, and the balloon will begin to inflate. The bottle may also become warm. After the hydrogen peroxide has stopped foaming, you will have a balloonful of oxygen!

What just happened?

Enzymes in the yeast cause hydrogen peroxide to decompose rapidly into water and oxygen. Since oxygen is a gas, it takes up more room than the original hydrogen peroxide liquid, so it expands into the balloon.

The hydrogen peroxide reaction is an **exothermic chemical reaction**, *which means that it releases chemical energy in the form of heat. Some chemical reactions absorb heat instead of releasing: they are called* **endothermic reactions**.

Chapter 3

Experiment #6

Shrinking Bottle

Supplies:
empty plastic water bottle

1. Screw the water bottle's cap on tightly. Place the bottle in the freezer for 10 minutes. Remove the water bottle. What happened?

2. Show a sibling, parent, or friend your experiment. Be sure to explain to the person *why* the sides of the bottle "caved in."

Experiment #7

Jumping Quarter

Supplies:
empty glass soda bottle
quarter

1. Put the empty glass bottle into the freezer.

2. After 10 minutes, remove the bottle and wet the mouth of the bottle with water. Place a quarter on top of the mouth of the bottle.

3. Now hold the bottle in your hands to warm the air inside the bottle. Within a few minutes, the quarter will begin to move and jump on top of the bottle. Can you explain *why* it does this? (Does matter expand or contract when it becomes warmer?)

Experiment #8

Can Crunch

 Do not attempt this experiment without adult supervision and/or assistance!

Supplies:
empty soda can
stove with exposed elements (not a glass-top stove)
tongs
bowl of cold water

1. Fill the empty soda can with two or three tablespoons of water. If you have an electric stove, place the can on the coils of the stove and turn the electric burner on high. If you have a gas stove, hold the can over the gas flame with tongs. In a few minutes the water will begin to boil inside the can. Let the water come to a rapid boil.

2. Using the tongs, lift the can off the burner. Immediately turn it over into the bowl of cold water. The can will "crunch" immediately, and water will be sucked up into the can.

What just happened?

When the water in the can boiled, it expanded into water vapor, or steam. This water vapor filled the can until there was no more air in the can.

When the can was placed upside down in the bowl of cold water, the water vapor in the can was cooled by the cold water in the bowl. The water vapor immediately condensed into droplets of liquid water.

Liquid water is about 1000 times denser than water vapor. This means that when water vapor condenses into a liquid, it becomes 1000 times smaller than it was as a gas. When the water vapor in the can condensed into liquid water droplets, the can condensed, or "crunched," along with it, and some of the water in the bowl was sucked up into the can to take the place of the water vapor.

Experiment #9

Freezing Points

Supplies:
ice cube tray
water
milk
oil
rubbing alcohol
salt water
soda pop or sugar water

1. Fill the top row of an ice cube tray with the following liquids, one in each space: water, milk, oil, rubbing alcohol, salt water, and soda pop or sugar water. Write labels for each liquid on small pieces of paper. Place the labels in the bottom row of the ice cube tray, arranging them so the label for milk is below the cube of milk, etc.

2. List the liquids in your Science Notebook in order of which you think will freeze first.

3. Put the ice cube tray in the freezer. Check the tray every hour and record which liquids freeze first. Leave the tray in the freezer overnight.

4. The next day, list the liquids in your Science Notebook again, this time in order of which actually froze first. Compare your predictions with what actually happened.

Experiment #10

Expanding Ice

Supplies:
plastic cup
water

Fill a plastic cup to the brim with water. Carefully place it in the freezer overnight. Record and explain the results in your Science Notebook.

Experiment #11

Gluten

Supplies:
½ cup water
1 cup flour
bowl

1. Put the flour into the bowl, stirring the water into the flour. Knead the dough for several minutes. Let the dough rest on the counter for about 10 minutes.

2. Hold the dough under the faucet and run cold water over it for about five minutes. As the starch is rinsed out of the dough, you will begin to see strands and webs of rubbery gluten. Continue rinsing the dough until the water is no longer cloudy. The rubbery ball that remains is pure gluten.

3. Share your ball of chewy gluten with family members who want to try it! Explain that gluten is the elastic protein that holds together cake, bread, and other baked goods.

Chapter 4

Experiment #12

Baking Soda-Vinegar Rocket

 Do not attempt this experiment without adult supervision!

When baking soda is combined with vinegar, the chemical energy in the baking soda is converted into mechanical energy. The chemical energy in baking soda is a form of potential energy, because it is energy that is not being used—it is energy "in storage," as it were. The mechanical energy of the expanding foam is a form of kinetic energy, or energy that is being used. In this experiment we will use the kinetic energy released by baking soda and vinegar to shoot off a cork rocket.

Supplies:
empty glass bottle with a cork (such as a wine bottle)
2 tablespoons baking soda
½ cup household vinegar

1. Pour ½ cup vinegar into the glass bottle. Measure two tablespoons of baking soda onto a tissue or piece of paper towel. Fold the tissue into a burrito-like package around the baking soda.

Complete the rest of the experiment outside in an open area. Make sure there is room for the cork to shoot out of the bottle without breaking anything. Never point the bottle towards yourself or another person!

2. When ready, slip the package of baking soda inside the bottle. Immediately seal the bottle with the cork, set the bottle upright on the ground, and move away from the bottle.

3. As the baking soda and vinegar react, the pressure on the cork will build up until the cork shoots out of the bottle. Estimate how high the cork travelled and record the distance in your Science Notebook. Do you think the cork would travel farther if you used more baking soda and vinegar? Try it!

Experiments : : Chapter 4

Experiment #13

Conductors and Insulators

Supplies:
rice sock or hot-and-cold pack (*not electric*)
3 kitchen utensils—1 plastic, 1 wood, and 1 metal—of similar lengths and with handles of similar thicknesses
3 large plastic drinking cups of similar sizes
water

1. Fill the three plastic cups with equal amounts of water. Put one utensil in each cup with the handles sticking out. Position each utensil so that its handle emerges from the water at the exact center of the cup. Use tape to keep the utensil in the correct position. Place the cups in the freezer until the water is frozen solid (overnight).

2. Take the cups of frozen ice out of the freezer and place them on their sides in a casserole dish or on a cookie sheet. Do not remove the ice from the cups.

3. Heat the rice sock or hot-and-cold pack. Lay the handles of the utensils on the rice sock or hot-and-cold pack so that each handle has the same amount of contact with the hot-and-cold pack. The hot-and-cold pack should be kept about two inches from the ice. You may wish to place the handles over the edge of the dish so the hot-and-cold pack will remain dry as the ice melts.

4. After 10 minutes, check to see if the ice around the handles has melted. If necessary, warm the hot-and-cold pack again. Check the experiment again after another 10 minutes. Record in your Science Notebook which handle has melted the most ice.

5. Interpret your results and draw conclusions. Which utensil—plastic, wood, or metal—conducted heat most efficiently from the hot-and-cold pack to the blocks of ice? Which of the materials—plastic, wood, or metal—are good conductors and which are good insulators?

Experiment #14

Convection Current

Supplies:
clear glass casserole dish
eyedropper or drinking straw
dye (milk can be used instead of dye)
water
3 coffee mugs of the same height

1. Fill the casserole dish with water (room temperature) and place it on top of two mugs. The mugs should be upright and positioned under each end of the casserole dish, leaving room for the third mug to be slipped between them beneath the center of the dish.

2. When the water in the dish has come to rest, use an eyedropper to release a small amount of dye at the bottom of the dish. Position the puddle of dye in the center of the dish. (You can use a plastic drinking straw instead of an eyedropper. Dip the straw into milk or dye and place your thumb over the top of the straw to keep the liquid from running out of the straw. Lower the straw to the bottom of the dish and release the milk or dye.)

3. Boil some water and pour it into the third mug. Without upsetting the water, gently slip the mug under the casserole dish, positioning it directly beneath the puddle of dye.

4. Within a few minutes, the heat from the boiling water will set up a convection current in the water. Look through the side of the casserole dish to view the convection current.

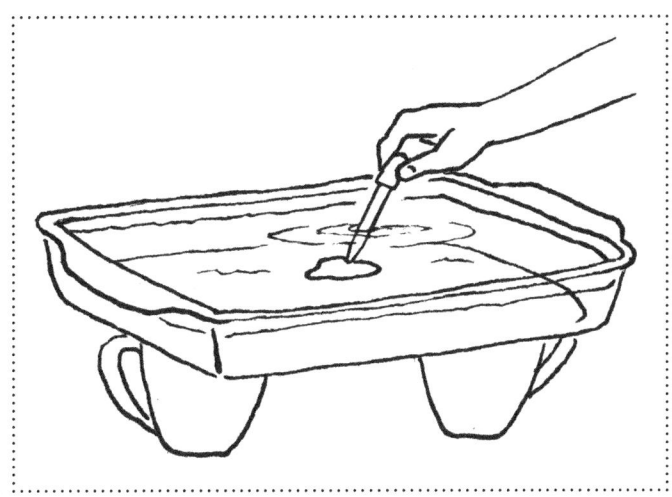

Chapter 5

Experiment #15
Fun with Static Electricity

Supplies:
2 balloons
wool garment
empty plastic bottle (water bottle, soda bottle, etc.)
scotch tape

1. Blow up a balloon and tie it off, then rub it on a wool garment. Electrons from the wool will "rub off" on the balloon, giving the balloon a negative charge. Repeat this step whenever the balloon's charge wears off.

2. See if you can make the balloon "stick" to the ceiling. Try using the balloon to attract hair. If you blow up another balloon and charge it with static electricity, will the balloons attract or repel each other?

3. Lay a plastic bottle on its side so it is free to roll. Bring the charged balloon near the bottle, then slowly move the balloon away from the bottle. The bottle should follow the balloon. See how fast you can make the bottle roll!

4. Stick the ends of two, four-inch pieces of scotch tape onto the edge of a desk. Quickly pull them off the desk, pulling straight out instead of up. Bring the ends of the tape towards each other. The pieces of tape became negatively charged when they were pulled off the table, so their ends should repel each other.

Experiment #16
More Fun with Static Electricity

Supplies:
balloon
wool garment
unflavored gelatin
rolled oats

1. Blow up a balloon and tie it off, then rub it on a wool garment. Electrons from the wool will "rub off" on the balloon, giving the balloon a negative charge. Repeat this step whenever the balloon's charge wears off.

2. Now sprinkle a layer of unflavored gelatin onto a plate. Gently bring your balloon close to the gelatin until it almost touches the plate. Observe the "gelatin stalactites" that are caused by the balloon's static electricity!

3. Pour some rolled oats onto a plate. Hold the charged balloon above the oats, and gradually bring it nearer to the plate. The oats will jump up and down between the plate and the balloon, because they are attracted by the extra electrons in the balloon. When enough electrons have traveled from the balloon to the oats, the oats fall back down to the plate.

4. Turn on the faucet so that a small stream of water pours out. Hold the charged balloon next to the stream of water, but do not let it touch the water. The stream of water will "bend" towards the balloon.

Experiment #17

Fun with Magnets

Supplies:
3 bar or horseshoe magnets (not refrigerator magnets) of similar strength
string
iron filings

1. Hang three magnets from strings and set one swinging. What effect does it have on the other magnets? Make sure the magnets are close enough that their magnetic fields influence each other, but not so close that they stick to each other.

2. Experiment with a magnet and iron filings to explore magnetic fields. Sprinkle a fine layer of iron filings onto a paper plate. Place your magnet underneath the plate, and watch the iron filings align themselves with the magnetic field. Move the magnet around and watch the iron filings follow it from one side of the plate to the other. If you have two magnets of different shapes, such as a bar magnet and a horseshoe magnet, compare the pattern each makes in the iron filings when it is placed underneath the plate.

If you don't have iron filings, you can collect them by running a magnet through dry soil or sand.

Experiment #18 (Optional)

Electrical Potential Difference

 Do not perform this experiment without the permission and assistance of a parent!

Supplies:
fluorescent light tube
balloon
wool garment

1. Ask a parent to remove the fluorescent light tube from its fixture. Your parent should hold the tube while you perform the experiment. **(Be very careful with the tube. Fluorescent light tubes implode when they are broken.)**

2. Blow up a balloon and give it a negative electric charge by rubbing it on the wool garment.

3. Touch the balloon to one end of the fluorescent light tube. The tube should flicker and glow for a few seconds. Don't worry—there is no danger of being electrocuted. One balloonful of static electricity is not powerful enough to do any harm.

What just happened?

Fluorescent light tubes give off light when loose electrons collide with the atoms inside the tube. To make electrons travel through the tube, you set up an electrical potential difference between the two ends of the tube. In other words, you made it so that one end of the tube had more electrons than the other end. When you touched the balloon to one end of the tube, the extra electrons on the balloon travelled through the tube, and the atoms in the tube gave off light.

Usually, a fluorescent light tube is attached to wires that connect it to a generator at a power plant. The generator sets up an electrical potential difference between the two ends of the light tube by providing one end of the light tube with extra electrons. The extra electrons on the negatively-charged side of the light tube are attracted to the positively-charged end of the light tube, so they travel through the tube, colliding with atoms as they go.

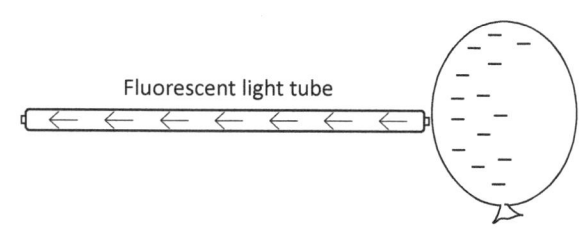

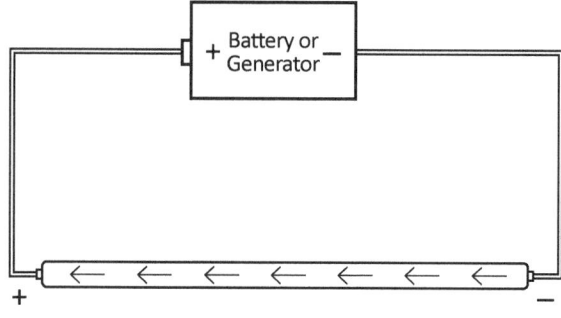

132 Experiments :: Chapter 5

Chapter 6

Experiment #19

Wheel and Axle

 This experiment requires the use of a sharp knife. Do not attempt it without your parent's permission and/or assistance!

Supplies:
large, raw potato, 2-3 inches in diameter
paring knife
string
a small weight (such as a bag or bucket of coins)
wooden pencil with flat sides

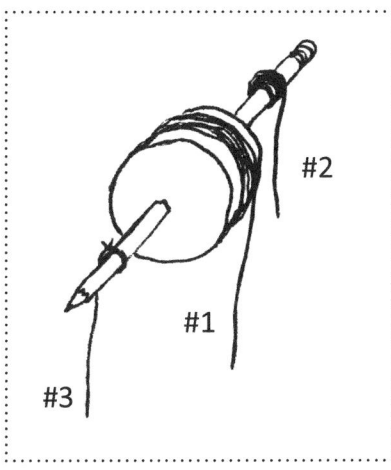

1. Wash the raw potato and slice off the ends until the potato is about two inches wide. Shape the potato with a knife or carrot peeler to make it as circular as possible. The goal is to form it into a round wheel with a diameter and width of about two inches.

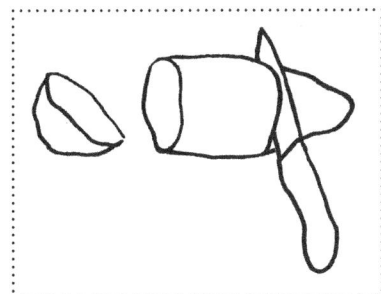

2. Stick a pencil through the center of your "potato-wheel." You may want to use a nail to pre-drill a hole. The pencil should fit inside the potato very tightly, so do not make the hole too big. The potato should not be able to rotate freely around the pencil. The potato is the wheel and the pencil is the axle in your homemade wheel-and-axle system.

3. Cut a four-foot-long piece of string. This will be string #1. Tie one end of string #1 tightly around the potato and wind the string around the potato as if the potato were a spool of thread.

4. Cut a two-foot-long piece of string. This will be string #2. Tie or tape one end of string #2 to the pencil, right next to the potato. If the string slips and rotates around the pencil, use a hot glue gun (with a parent's permission) to fasten it. Wind the string around the pencil. String #1 and string #2 should be wound in the same direction.

5. Cut another two-foot-long piece of string. This will be string #3. Tie or tape (or hot glue) one end of string #3 to the pencil, on the other side of the potato. Attach a weight (perhaps a small bag of coins) to the end of this string.

Experiments : : Chapter 6   133

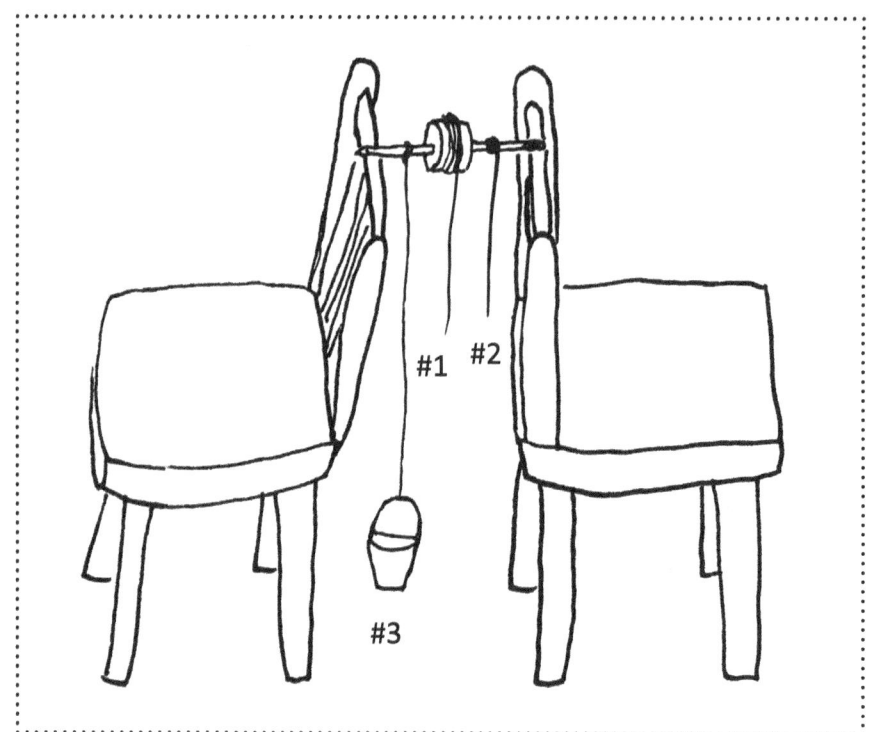

6. Hang the pencil between two chairs so that it can rotate freely. Pull down on string #2. As string #2 unwinds from the pencil, string #3 will be wound onto the pencil in the opposite direction. Keep pulling on string #2 until the weight at the end of string #3 has been raised four inches. Measure how much of string #2 has been unwound from the pencil and record the length in your Science Notebook.

7. Unwind string #3 and wind string #2 back onto the pencil. Now pull down on string #1. Keep pulling until the weight at the end of string #3 has been raised four inches. Measure how much of string #1 has been unwound from the pencil and record the length in your Science Notebook.

8. Interpret the results and draw conclusions by answering the following questions in your Science Notebook.

   - *Did it take more effort to raise the weight by pulling on the string attached to the axle (string #2) or by pulling on the string attached to the wheel (string #1)?*

   - *Which string did you have to pull the farthest: the string attached to the axle (string #2) or the string attached to the wheel (string #1)?*

   - *Is this consistent with what you have learned in your textbook about the wheel and axle?*

Experiment #20

Simple and Fixed Pulleys

 This experiment requires the use of a sharp knife. Do not attempt it without your parent's permission and/or assistance!

Supplies:

string

2 large, raw potatoes

2 pencils with smooth sides

small weight (such as a bag or bucket of coins)

sharp knife

1. Wash the potatoes and slice off the ends until each potato is about two inches wide. Shape each potato with a knife or carrot peeler to form it into a round wheel.

2. Cut a ¼-inch wedge around each "potato-wheel," as shown in Figure 1. Make this cut as straight and smooth as possible, making sure there is an equal amount of potato on each side of the wedge.

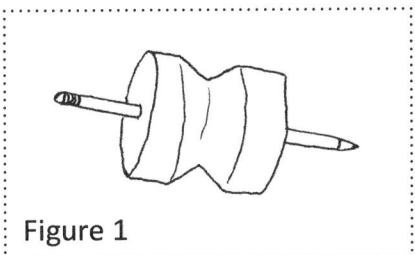

Figure 1

3. Stick a pencil through the center of each potato-wheel. You may want to use a nail to pre-drill a hole. The pencils should fit inside the potatoes very *loosely*, so that the potatoes can rotate freely around the pencils. Each potato-on-a-pencil is a homemade pulley.

Fixed Pulley

4. Hang one of the potato-pulleys between two chairs, with one side of the pencil on the back of each chair. Secure the pencil to the chairs, making sure that the potato can still rotate freely around the pencil. Cut a long piece of string—perhaps four to five feet—and tie one end of it to the small weight. Lay the string over the potato-pulley so that the string rests in the potato's wedge. (See Figure 2.)

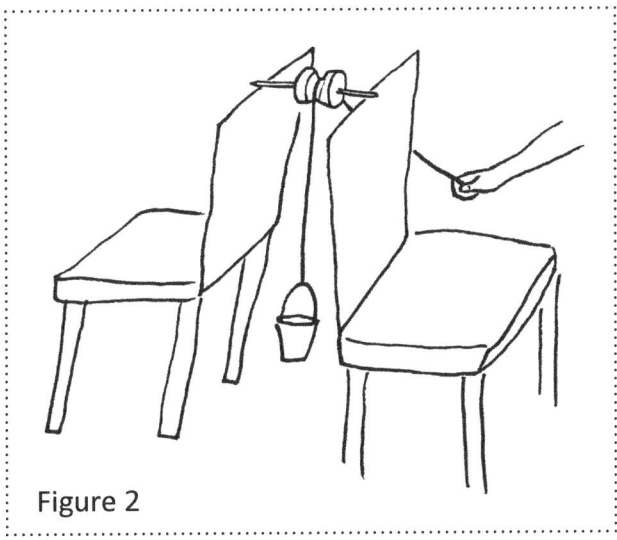

Figure 2

5. You've just made a fixed pulley! Pull down on the loose end of the string to lift the weight on the other side of the pulley. Test how far you have to pull the loose end of the string to raise the weight one foot. Does the weight feel heavier, lighter, or the same when lifted with the pulley? Record your results in your Science Notebook.

Moveable Pulley

6. Now use the other potato-pulley to make a moveable pulley. Cut six to eight inches of string, and attach the weight to the very center of the string. Tie the ends of the string to one of the pencils, with one end of the string on either side of the potato-wheel. (For a sturdier moveable pulley, you could use six to eight inches of wire instead of string.) The string and pencil should form an upside-down triangle with the pencil as the flat top of the triangle.

7. Attach four to five feet of string to a door handle, the back of a chair, or another sturdy object. Thread the string through the upside-down triangle, so that your moveable pulley hangs from the string. (See Figure 3.) Pull up on the loose end of the string to lift

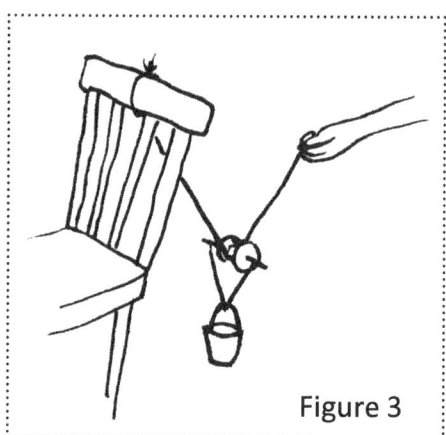

Figure 3

the weight that is attached to the moveable pulley. The potato-wheel should roll along the string as you raise or lower the string. Test how far you have to pull the loose end of the string to raise the weight one foot. Does the weight feel heavier, lighter, or the same when lifted with the pulley? Record your results in your Science Notebook.

Fixed and Moveable Pulleys

8. Now combine the fixed pulley and the

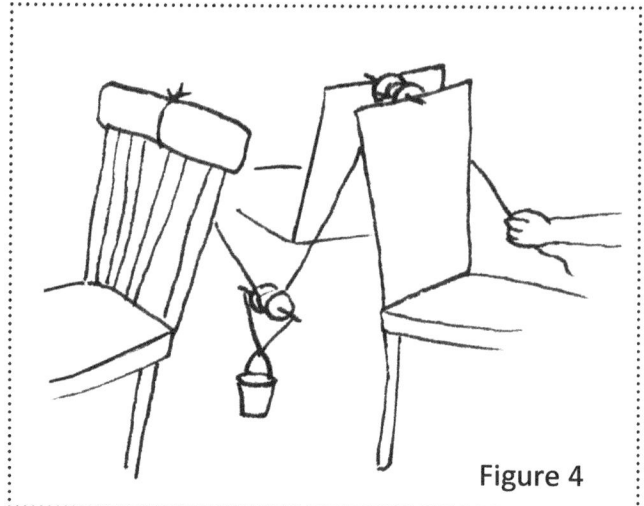

Figure 4

moveable pulley by laying the loose end of the string over your fixed pulley. (See Figure 4.) Pull down on the loose end of the string to lift the weight that is attached to the moveable pulley. Test how far you have to pull the loose end of the string to raise the weight one foot. Does the weight feel heavier, lighter, or the same as it did when you lifted it with just a moveable pulley? Record your results in your Science Notebook.

9. Interpret your results and draw conclusions by answering the following questions in your Science Notebook.

- *Did it take more effort to raise the weight with a fixed pulley or a moveable pulley?*
- *How much farther did you have to pull the string when you used a moveable pulley instead of a fixed pulley?*
- *When you use a fixed pulley and a moveable pulley instead of just a moveable pulley, did you have to pull the string farther?*
- *Did the combination of fixed pulley and moveable pulley make the weight feel less heavy?*
- *Are your results consistent with what you have learned in your textbook about pulleys?*

Chapter 8

Experiment #21

Frozen Celery Cells

Supplies:
stalk of celery

1. Place the stalk of celery in the freezer until it is frozen solid, approximately 2 hours.

2. Remove the celery from the freezer. Leave the celery at room temperature until it is thawed, and then examine it carefully. In your Science Notebook, describe the appearance of the thawed celery. Can you explain what happened?

Experiment #22

Parabolic Solar Heater

Supplies:
3-4 large, round kitchen bowls
aluminum foil
direct sunlight

1. Cover the inside of the bowl with aluminum foil. The shiny side of the foil should be facing out.

2. Set the bowl in direct sunlight. Prop the bowl on its side so it faces directly into the Sun. After a few minutes, feel the air at the bottom of the bowl. Is it warmer than the air outside the bowl? Record the results of your experiment in your Science Notebook.

3. Repeat the experiment with two or three other bowls. Does one of the bowls heat the air better than the others? What does this tell you about the shape of the bowl?

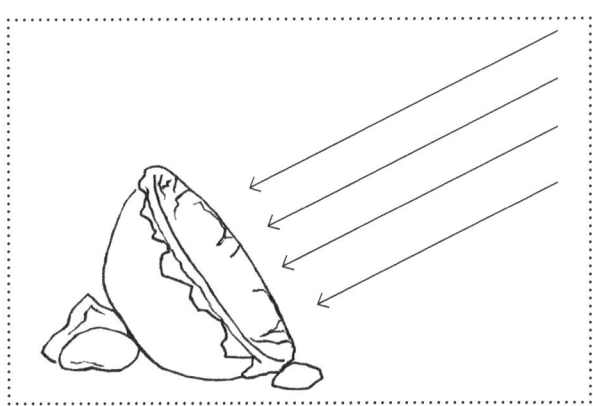

Your bowl is not a perfect parabola, but it should still reflect sunlight towards the center of the bowl. By covering the bowl with aluminum foil, you are making sure the Sun's rays are reflected towards the center of the bowl instead of being absorbed by the bowl itself. The petals of tundra plants are not covered with aluminum foil, but they still reflect sunlight towards the center of the flowers. Any sunshine that is not reflected is absorbed by the flower, which helps keep the plant warm.

Chapter 9

Experiment #23

Plant Obstacle Course

Supplies:
packet of bean seeds
large container for planting (dish or potting tray)
small container (plastic cup, small pot, the bottom of an empty water bottle)
soil
water
shoebox (or a similar box)
brown cardboard (or another dark color—cardboard with a white finish will reflect the light)
tape
scissors
rubber band

1. Fill the large dish or container with moist soil. Plant 12 bean seeds in the container, following the instructions on the seed packet. Water the seeds lightly. Place the container indoors in a sunny location. Set aside one or two pages in your Science Notebook for this experiment, and record the date on which you planted the seeds.

2. Water the seeds regularly to keep the soil damp, but be careful not to drown them. The beans should sprout in five to seven days. When they sprout, record the date in your Science Notebook. Continue caring for the beans until at least a few have their second set of leaves, about 10-12 days after they were first planted.

3. Cut out two pieces of cardboard and tape them into the shoebox to form two shelves (see above). Cut a one-inch hole in one end of the shoebox, and seal up any other holes. Set the shoebox on its end so the one-inch hole is on top.

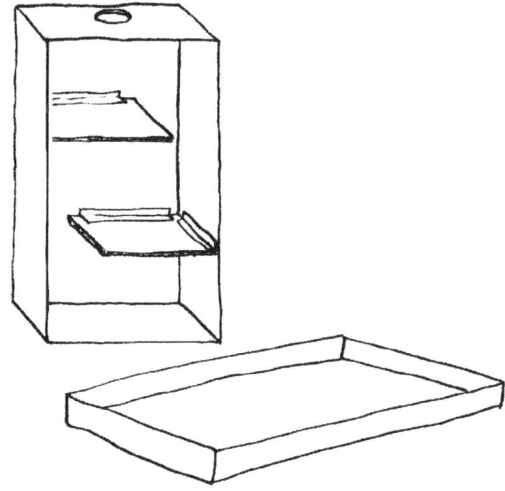

4. Transplant the largest, healthiest bean plant into the small container, being careful not to tear the plant's roots. Water it lightly, then place it inside the shoebox, underneath the first cardboard shelf. **Note: do not throw away the other bean plants. They will be used in Experiment #25.**

5. Close the lid of the shoebox and stretch a rubber band around it to make sure the lid does not fall off. Place the box indoors in a sunny location. In your Science Notebook, record the date on which you transplanted the bean plant into the shoebox obstacle course.

6. Check on your bean plant every day, watering it regularly to keep the soil damp. Do not overwater. Like all plants, beans need sunlight to live, so your bean plant will grow rapidly to find its way to the light. You may wish to take a photo of the plant every day.

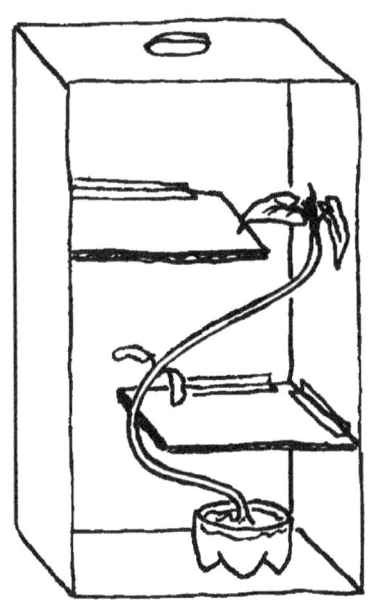

7. Within two or three weeks, your bean plant will have reached the light and be growing through the hole in the top of the shoebox. Record the date in your Science Notebook. How long did it take the bean to find its way through the obstacle course?

Sunlight is so important for plants that God has given them the ability to grow towards the light. This ability is called "phototropism," which means "turning towards the light." Being on the forest floor of the rainforest is like being in a dark shoebox—except that a plant has to grow much farther to reach the light! Small plants in the rainforest are unable to do this, which is why most of them grow on the branches of trees high in the air.

Experiments : : Chapter 9

Experiment #24

Needles and Broad Leaves

Supplies:
paper towels
water
waxed paper
sunshine or a warm room

1. Tear off three paper towel sheets. Soak them in water from the faucet and squeeze them out lightly.

2. Spread the three paper towels out on a flat surface, then roll two of them up like tubes. Wrap one of the paper-towel tubes in a sheet of waxed paper.

3. Lay the three paper towels outdoors on a sunny deck, sidewalk, or other surface. Spread the first paper towel out flat, but keep the second and third paper towels rolled up like tubes. (Depending on the weather, you may wish to perform the experiment inside. In that case, spread the paper towels out in a warm room. Do not place them near a heater or fireplace.) The first paper towel represents the broad leaf of an oak or maple tree, and the second and third paper towels represent the needles of evergreen conifers.

4. After 30 minutes, check to see which paper towel is most dry. Check them again every 30 minutes. Which paper towel dried out first? Which paper towel remained wet the longest? Record your findings in your Science Notebook.

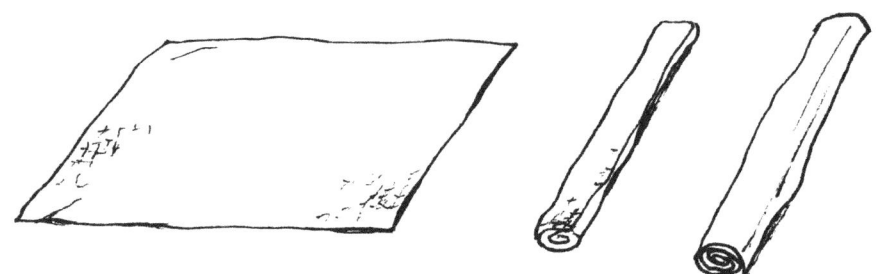

The paper towel that is laid out flat demonstrates how quickly water evaporates from broad leaves. The paper towels that are rolled up show how the shape of conifer needles keeps water from evaporating as quickly. The paper towel that is rolled up and wrapped in waxed paper shows how a waxy coating makes conifer needles even better at conserving water.

Chapter 10

Experiment #25

Rainforest Soil

Supplies:
bucket
watering can or hose
water
1-2 shovelfuls of soil
cheesecloth, thin fabric, screen, or sieve
2 bean plants of the same size that look equally healthy, saved from Experiment #23

1. Put ⅔ of the soil onto the cheesecloth, screen, or sieve and place it over the bucket. With the help of a parent, sibling, or friend, carefully pour water over the soil with a hose or watering can. Gently stir the soil with your fingers as you pour the water. When the bucket is full of water, remove the cheesecloth and soil. The water in the bucket will be clouded and brown because it is full of nutrients and minerals that have been washed, or *leached*, out of the soil. You may also find a layer of clay or silt at the bottom of the bucket.

2. Dump out the water in the bucket, and repeat step 1 several times, using fresh water and the same soil. Each time you pour the water through the soil, examine the water in the bucket. You should notice that the water does not get as brown as it did at first.

3. Continue pouring water through the soil until the water in the bucket is almost clear. You may need to rinse the soil a dozen times. The soil has now been leached of most of its nutrients and minerals. Gently squeeze out the soil and place it in a small cup or pot.

4. Select two of the bean plants you saved from Experiment #23. The plants should be of the same size and look equally healthy. Gently remove one of the bean plants from its soil and brush the soil out of the roots. Be careful not to tear the roots. Transplant the bean plant into the cup of leached soil and place it indoors on a windowsill or other sunny location.

5. Fill the second cup or pot with regular, unleached soil. Transplant the second bean plant into the cup of unleached soil, carefully brushing the soil from the roots. Again, be careful not to tear the roots. Place it next to the first bean plant. You can now plant the extra bean plants from Experiment #23 in the garden. They will not be needed for further experiments.

6. Label the two pots so you remember which is which, and then leave the two bean plants in the windowsill, watering them whenever the soil feels dry. After about a one or two weeks, answer the following questions in your Science Notebook. *Which plant grew the most? Which one looks healthier than the other? What do the results of the experiment tell you about the effect of heavy rainfall on the soil?*

Chapter 16

Experiment #26

Greenhouse Effect

Like greenhouse gases in the atmosphere, glass allows rays of sunshine to pass through it, but blocks the passage of infrared radiation (heat rays). Many plastics work the same way. In this experiment, you will see how a layer of plastic wrap can turn a bowl of water into a heat trap.

Supplies:
2 small bowls, of similar size and material
plastic wrap
water
direct sunlight

1. Fill the two bowls with cool tap water. Cover one bowl tightly with plastic wrap.

2. Place both bowls of water in direct sunlight, and leave them there for 30 minutes to an hour. Make sure the bowls are resting on the same type of surface and receive the same amount of sunlight.

3. After about 30 minutes, feel the temperature of the water in each bowl. Is one warmer than the other? If you don't notice a significant difference, leave the bowls in direct sunlight for another 30 minutes, and then compare the temperatures again.

4. Show your experiment to a parent, sibling, or friend, and explain why one bowl is warmer than the other.

ANSWER KEY

UNIT 1

Chapter 2

WORD SCRAMBLE, pg. 1
1. mass
2. volume
3. density
4. science

FILL IN THE BLANK, pg. 1
1. volume
2. science
3. mass
4. density

DENSITY AND THE BUOYANT FORCE, pg. 2
1. less dense
2. more matter in a cubic inch of water
3. sink, float
4. more, less
5. more, push it down

WHAT IS TRUE?, pg. 3
1. True
2. True
3. False
4. True
5. False
6. False
7. True

ELEMENT, COMPOUND, OR MIXTURE?, pg. 4
1. Compound
2. Element
3. Mixture
4. compound
5. element
6. element
7. compound

CLASSIFYING MATTER, pg. 5
1. pure substances, mixtures
2. elements, compounds
3. physical
4. chemical

ATOMS, pg. 6
1. empty space
2. protons, neutrons
3. protons, neutrons, electrons

LABEL THE PARTS OF AN ATOM, pg. 6
4. proton (or neutron)
5. electron
6. neutron (or proton)
7. nucleus

CHAPTER 2 REVIEW, pgs. 7-8
1. Yes, the volume of an object can change even when its mass stays the same.
2. Observation, question, hypothesis, method, interpretation, conclusion
3. Density is the measurement of how much matter is packed into a certain space.
4. The buoyant force is the upward "push" which water (or any other liquid) gives to objects.
5. An atom is a tiny particle, the basic building block of matter.
6. An element is a substance made of only one type of atom.
7. A compound is a substance made of only one type of molecule.
8. Molecules are tiny particles formed when two or more atoms are chemically "glued" together in a particular position.
9. A mixture is made out of any number of different atoms and molecules arranged in any order.
10. A pure substance is matter that consists of only one type of particle.
11. The nucleus of an atom is its center, which is made up of protons and neutrons.
12. Electrons are smaller particles that are constantly whizzing around the nucleus.

Chapter 3

LIQUID, SOLID, OR GAS?, pg. 9
1. energy
2. thermal
3. gaseous state
4. freezing
5. melting
6. condensation
7. solid
8. liquid
9. solid
10. gas
11. liquid

FILL IN THE BLANKS, pg. 10
1. sublimation
2. deposition
3. condensation
4. vaporization
5. melting
6. freezing

SOLUBILITY, pg. 11
1. solutions
2. Solvent
3. soluble
4. insoluble
5. saturated
6. universal solvent

CHAPTER 3 REVIEW, pgs. 12-13
1. Matter changes from one state to another because of a change in energy.
2. Atoms and molecules become more energetic when they are heated.
3. Evaporation is the type of vaporization that occurs when "speedy," energetic particles burst through the surface of the liquid and escape into the air.
4. Condensation is the process in which a gas is turned into a liquid.
5. Water freezes at 32°F.
6. Water boils at 212°F.
7. expands, contracts

8. Water expands when it is frozen because the water molecules arrange themselves in ice crystals, and ice crystals take up more room than liquid water.
9. Solubility is the ability of one material to be dissolved into another.
10. i. b., ii. c., iii. a.

Chapter 4

WORD SCRAMBLE, pg. 14
1. sweep
2. hopscotch
3. brushing
4. walk
5. fishing
6. toss
7. rowing
8. climb
9. rake

FILL IN THE BLANK, pg. 14
Work, force

CLASSIFY ENERGY, pg. 15
1. chemical
2. chemical
3. mechanical
4. mechanical
5. thermal
6. mechanical
7. thermal
8. mechanical
9. thermal
10. chemical

ENERGY TRANSFORMATION, pg. 16
1. thermal
2. mechanical
3. mechanical
4. thermal
5. mechanical
6. mechanical
7. mechanical
8. thermal

POTENTIAL AND KINETIC ENERGY, pg. 17
1. potential
2. kinetic
3. potential
4. kinetic
5. potential
6. kinetic
7. kinetic
8. potential
9. kinetic

THE SENSATION OF HEAT AND CONDUCTION, pg. 18
1. Heat (or thermal energy)
2. thermal energy
3. conduction
4. brought into direct contact
5. conductors, metal
6. insulators; plastic, fabric, wood, or air

CONVECTION AND RADIATION, pg. 19
1. conduction, convection, radiation
2. convection
3. dense
4. infrared
5. objects
6. thermal energy
7. it is so cold in comparison with other objects.

CHAPTER 4 REVIEW, pgs. 20-21
1. Energy is the ability to do work.
2. Work occurs whenever a force moves an object to a new location.
3. Mechanical energy is the energy that is used to do work.
4. Thermal energy is the energy that makes atoms and molecules move and jiggle.
5. Chemical energy is the energy that is released when atoms and molecules react with each other.
6. Potential energy is energy that is not being used, but could be.
7. Kinetic energy is energy that is being used.
8. Conduction is the transfer of thermal energy through atoms and molecules bumping into each other.
9. An insulator is a material that doesn't "pass on" thermal energy very well. Conductors are materials that are particularly good at "passing on" thermal energy.
10. Convection is the transfer of thermal energy by means of circulating liquids and gases.
11. Radiation is a way of transferring heat and light through electromagnetic waves.
12. Infrared rays are the invisible waves of energy that are radiated by an object such as a hot clothes iron.
13. *At least three of the following:* X-rays, radio waves, rays of visible light (sunlight), infrared rays, microwaves

Chapter 5

FILL IN THE BLANKS, pg. 22
1. electrons, protons, neutrons
2. Electrons
3. Static electricity
4. protons
5. electrons, protons
6. protons, electrons
7. attract, repel
8. static electrical discharge
9. air, water vapor

WHAT IS TRUE?, pg. 23
1. False
2. False
3. False
4. True
5. False
6. False
7. True
8. False
9. The proton will travel towards the balloon.

145

FILL IN THE BLANKS, pg. 24
1. potential
2. kinetic
3. no
4. potential
5. electric current
6. Electrons
7. generator
8. current
9. energy
10. electrons
11. battery (or generator)
12. generator (or battery)

MORE ABOUT ELECTRICITY, pg. 25
1. Electrical potential difference
2. protons, electrons
3. attraction
4. battery, generator
5. slowly
6. work
7. something, nothing
8. coulomb
9. ampere
10. volt

CHAPTER 5 REVIEW, pgs. 26-28
1. The most important fact about charges is that unlike charges attract and like charges repel.
2. Nick's hair was standing on end because all his hairs had a positive charge, so each hair was repelled by the other hairs.
3. Induced magnetism is the type of magnetism that magnetic materials have when they are in contact with a magnet.
4. A magnetic field is the region in which a magnet's "pull" can be felt by magnetic materials.
5. An electric field is the region in which the "push" or "pull" of an electron or proton can be felt by other particles.
6. An electric current is the flow of millions of electrons through an electrical wire.
7. An electrical potential difference is a difference in charge between two materials.
8. Electrons move in an ordinary wire at about four inches per hour.
9. The push of energy from a generator or battery moves through a wire in less than a second.
10. The Law of Conservation of Energy states that we can't get something for nothing.
11. The term "watt" measures how much electrical power a certain appliance uses.
12. c
13. e
14. a
15. f
16. b
17. h
18. d
19. g

Chapter 6

WHAT IS TRUE?, pg. 29
1. False
2. True
3. False
4. False
5. True
6. True
7. False
8. Examples will vary.

FILL IN THE BLANKS, pg. 30
1. fulcrum
2. up
3. direction
4. closer
5. large, long
6. distance, distance

FIRST, SECOND, AND THIRD CLASS LEVERS, pg. 31
1. a) force
   b) load
   c) fulcrum
2. a) force
   b) fulcrum
   c) load
3. a) load
   b) force
   c) fulcrum

WHAT IS TRUE?, pg. 32
1. True
2. True
3. False
4. False
5. True
6. True
7. True
8. False
9. False

WHEELS MAKE WORK EASIER, pg. 33
1. Friction
2. rolling wheel
3. wheel and axle
4. full
5. work
6. distance
7. reverse
8. distance

WHEELS, pg. 34
1. wheel and axle
2. wheel and axle
3. rolling wheels
4. rolling wheels
5. wheel and axle
6. wheel and axle
7. rolling wheels
8. wheel and axle

PULLEYS, pg. 35
1. moveable
2. fixed
3. direction
4. multiplies
5. C, D
6. True
7. False
8. True

CHAPTER 6 REVIEW, pgs. 36-37
1. An inclined plane is a simple machine that allows us to raise objects little by little instead of all at once.
2. A screw is a special type of inclined plane that can convert a rotational movement into a vertical movement.
3. A wedge is a simple machine made out of two inclined planes placed back to back.
4. A lever is a long board or rod that rotates around a fulcrum.
5. A wheel and axle is a simple machine made of a wheel firmly attached to a rod or smaller wheel.
6. A pulley is a wheel in a frame.
7. A fixed pulley is attached to the ceiling; it changes the direction of a force.
8. A moveable pulley is free to move; it reduces the force needed to lift the load.
9. A fulcrum is a sturdy object or surface that a lever rotates around.
10. Friction is the "drag" that we feel when we move objects across each other.
11. crowbar
12. tongs
13. crowbar
14. stairs
15. broom
16. hammer
17. oars
18. nail

Unit 1 Test

pgs. 38-39
1. b
2. a
3. a
4. b
5. a
6. c
7. b
8. c
9. b
10. a
11. b
12. c
13. a, b
14. a
15. a

UNIT 2

Chapter 7

RELATIONSHIPS, pg. 41
1. predator : prey = predatory
2. prey : predator = predatory
3. facilitative
4. parasite : host = parasitic
5. predator : prey = predatory
6. facilitative
7. predator : prey = predatory

FOOD CHAINS, pg. 42
1. kingfisher, trout, tadpole, algae
2. mountain lion, deer, bush
3. Secondary Consumers
4. Primary Consumers
5. Primary Producers: Plants, Algae, and Deep-Sea Bacteria
6. Dead organic material, which worms, insects, bacteria, and fungi decompose into . . .

BIOMES MAP, pg. 43
1. Answers will vary.
2. c
3. b
4. c
5. a
6. d
7. c
8. c

MATCH-UP, pg. 44
1. E
2. J
3. B
4. N
5. F
6. K
7. H
8. L
9. A
10. D
11. C
12. G
13. M
14. I

Chapter 8

THINKING ABOUT THE CHAPTER, PART 1, pg. 46
1. In the summer, the North Pole is tilted towards the Sun, so the Sun never sets for locations near the North Pole.
2. Trees can't grow in the tundra because permafrost, a layer of permanently frozen soil, keeps them from sinking their roots into the soil.
3. During the winter, lemmings live in long tunnels between the snow and the ground, where they can nibble on the roots and leaves of snow-covered plants.
4. Most tundra animals do not hibernate during the winter because eight to ten months is too long for most of them to survive in a state of hibernation.
5. Freeze-avoidant insects produce chemicals such as glycerol that lower the freezing temperature of their body fluids. The insects' bodies can be as cold as the sub-zero snow and winds around them, but still not freeze.

RELATIONSHIPS & FOOD CHAINS, pg. 47
1. prey : predator = predatory
2. host : parasite = parasitic
3. facilitative
4. predator : prey = predatory
5. facilitative
6. prey : predator = predatory
7. roots/leaves, snowy owl/arctic fox
8. caribou, birds

THINKING ABOUT THE CHAPTER, PART 2, pg. 48

1. Tundra plants are short because they depend on the snow to insulate them from the freezing air, and the snow is often only a few inches deep in the tundra.

2. Answers will vary.

3. Caribou have special bacteria in their stomachs that help them break down the complex carbohydrates and nutrients in lichens.

4. Lichen is formed from two different creatures: fungi and algae. The algae part of the lichen produces energy through photosynthesis. In return, the fungus absorbs water and minerals for the algae to use and provides the algae with a secure place to live.

CHAPTER 8 REVIEW, pg. 49

1. False
2. True
3. True
4. False
5. True
6. False
7. True
8. False
9. False
10. False
11. True
12. False

Chapter 9

THINKING ABOUT THE CHAPTER, PART 1, pg. 51

1. The soil in the boreal forest is poor because the acidic needles of conifer trees require a long time to decompose. The cold temperatures during much of the year delay decomposition even further, because it is difficult for worms, insects, fungi, and bacteria to decompose the soil without warm weather.

2. Bogs form over standing water, but fens receive water and nutrients from surrounding streams or groundwater. Fens contain a greater variety of plants than do bogs, which are dominated by sphagnum moss. Fens are also much more treacherous than bogs are.

3. To make a lodge, beavers first pile up a huge mound of sticks and mud. Then they dig and chew a tunnel in the mound, beginning underwater and moving towards the top of the mound. When their tunnel rises above the water level, they expand it into a large chamber.

4. Beavers work all summer to store up a huge pile of branches underwater near their lodge. In the winter, they swim under the ice from their lodge to their store of food, and eat the twigs and small branches.

RELATIONSHIPS AND FOOD CHAINS, pg. 52

1. predator : prey = predatory
2. facilitative
3. host : parasite = parasitic
4. predator : prey = predatory
5. prey : predator = predatory
6. Answers will vary. Examples include the lynx, fox, wolf, fisher, etc.
7. pine nuts

THINKING ABOUT THE CHAPTER, PART 2, pg. 53

1. Answers may vary, but should include at least three of the following: 1) The pointed shape of conifers helps keep their branches from cracking under the weight of a heavy snowfall. 2) Evergreen trees don't have to produce a whole new set of leaves each spring, so they don't require as many nutrients as deciduous trees. 3) Evergreen trees are able to start photosynthesizing in the spring immediately, instead of having to grow new leaves first. 4) The dark green color of most evergreens allows them to absorb more of the Sun's warmth. 5) Conifer needles are better at conserving, or saving, water than broad leaves are.

2. Fires decompose the organic material on the forest floor, making the ground rich and fertile. Fires clear the ground for new growth and ensure that new seedlings have plenty of light. Fires purify forests of diseases and parasitic insects.

3. Carnivorous plants capture insects because they grow in poor soil and need another source of nutrients.

4. Salmon are born in freshwater rivers, spend most of their lives in the salty ocean, and then return to freshwater rivers to lay their eggs and die.

CHAPTER 9 REVIEW, pg. 54

1. True
2. False
3. True
4. True
5. True
6. False
7. True
8. False
9. True
10. False
11. True
12. True
13. True
14. True
15. True

Chapter 10

THINKING ABOUT THE CHAPTER, PART 1, pg. 57

1. Reptiles and amphibians need the warmth of the Sun to remain active, so they have to hibernate underground during the winter. This is why it is difficult for them to live

in biomes where the winter is extremely long.

2. The temperature in the rainforest remains the same throughout the year because tropical rainforests are situated near the Equator.

3. The soil is poor in tropical rainforests because the constant, heavy rainfall washes nutrients and minerals out of the soil.

4. Small rainforest plants would not get enough sunlight if they grew on the forest floor. Instead, they grow high above the ground on the branches of trees where there is plenty of sunlight.

RELATIONSHIPS AND FOOD CHAINS, pg. 58

1. facilitative
2. predator : prey = predatory
3. facilitative
4. parasite : host = parasitic
5. predator : prey = predatory
6. facilitative
7. predator : prey = predatory
8. Answers will vary.
9. agouti

THINKING ABOUT THE CHAPTER, PART 2, pg. 59

1. Deep in the rainforest, the forest floor does not receive enough sunlight for many plants to grow on the ground. On the edge of rivers and clearings the forest receives more sunlight, so there is also more undergrowth.

2. Many species are able to live and flourish in the rainforest because each creature has a very specific niche and habitat. This is because specialization allows each creature to find unique sources of food and reduce competition with other animals.

3. Answers may vary, but most examples are discussed in section 10.6 of the text.

4. Answers may vary, but most examples are discussed in section 10.7 of the text.

CHAPTER 10 REVIEW, pg. 60

1. False
2. True
3. False
4. True
5. False
6. True
7. False
8. True
9. False
10. False
11. True
12. False
13. False
14. False
15. True

Chapter 11

THINKING ABOUT THE CHAPTER, PART 1, pg. 62

1. Very few trees grow on the prairie because prairie fires and the grazing of large animals prevent seedlings from growing into mature trees.

2. The dung beetle is important to life in the African savanna because it buries dung all over the savanna. This prevents the dung from hardening and killing the grass beneath it, and it also enriches the soil, because dung is a powerful fertilizer.

3. The tunneling of termites mixes and loosens the ground, and their droppings enrich the soil. Eagles, cheetahs, and mongooses use termite mounds as lookouts, and smaller animals rest in their shade. A termite mound is a source of food for aardvarks and birds and it is a back scratcher for elephants. Deserted termite mounds provide homes for snakes, foxes, warthogs, and other species.

RELATIONSHIPS AND FOOD CHAINS, pg. 64

1. facilitative
2. prey : predator = predatory
3. predator : prey = predatory
4. predator : prey = predatory
5. prey : predator = predatory
6. grass, snake
7. Answers will vary. Examples include the lion, leopard, cheetah, etc.

THINKING ABOUT THE CHAPTER, PART 2, pg. 65

1. Large ears help desert animals to cool off because the air that flows across the bare skin of the ear cools the animal's blood. The larger its ears are, the more blood it can cool at a time. Slender bodies with long, narrow limbs naturally lose heat more quickly than chubby, round bodies.

2. Answers will vary.

3. Cacti grow shallow, spreading roots that immediately soak up the moisture of any rainfall. Trees and shrubs sink deep tap roots as far as 100 feet to reach underground water sources.

4. If a plant's seeds sprout right next to the parent plant, they will not be able to survive because the roots of the mature plant will absorb all the water.

CHAPTER 11 REVIEW, pg. 66

1. True
2. True
3. False
4. False
5. True
6. True
7. True
8. False
9. True
10. True
11. False
12. True
13. False
14. False
15. True
16. True

Chapter 12

WHAT IS TRUE?, pg. 67
1. True
2. False
3. True
4. True
5. False
6. True
7. True
8. False
9. True
10. True

FILL IN THE BLANKS #1, pg. 68
1. seed
2. suppress
3. crowded
4. Controlled
5. harvesting
6. lumber
7. renewable
8. recycled
9. petroleum

FILL IN THE BLANKS #2, pg. 69
1. selective
2. genes
3. genetically

WHAT IS TRUE?, pg. 69
1. False
2. True
3. True
4. False

Unit 2 Test

pgs. 70-71
1. c
2. b
3. c
4. b
5. c
6. c
7. c
8. d
9. b
10. a
11. b
12. d
13. c
14. b
15. a
16. c
17. b
18. c

UNIT 3

Chapter 13

DISTANCES AND APPEARANCES, pg. 74
1. True
2. False
3. False
4. True
5. False
6. False
7. False
8. farther from
9. closer to

WHAT IS TRUE?, pg. 75
1. True
2. False
3. True
4. False

ROTATION AND REVOLUTION, pgs. 75-76
1. revolve
2. Pole
3. Equator
4. Merak
5. rotation
6. Ursa Minor
7. north
8. Big Dipper
9. Cassiopeia
10. axis
11. circle
12. Polaris

FILL IN THE BLANK, pg. 76
rotating, axis

CHAPTER 13 REVIEW, pgs. 77-78
1. Astronomy is the scientific study of the stars, the planets, and all the other objects in outer space.
2. A constellation is a group of stars that makes a picture.
3. A light-year is the distance light can travel in a year, about six trillion miles.
4. An AU, or astronomical unit, is the distance between the Earth and the Sun, about 93 million miles.
5. To rotate means to spin.
6. To revolve means to travel in a circle around something else.
7. Polaris is special because it never moves, all night long.
8. We see different parts of the sky all night long because the Earth is rotating on its axis.
9. We see different stars at different times of the year because the Earth is revolving around the Sun.
10. One fist-width equals 10° and one finger-width equals 1°. Latitude is the way that scientists measure a location's distance from the Equator.
11. Huck Finn has been asleep for three hours.

Chapter 14

GRAVITY AND ORBITS, pg. 79
1. False
2. True
3. True
4. True
5. True
6. True
7. True
8. True
9. False
10. False
11. True
12. True

LUNAR PHASES, pg. 80
1. orbits
2. crescent
3. gibbous
4. tilt
5. planets
6. waxing
7. full moon
8. waning

FILL IN THE BLANK, pg. 80
orbiting

MORE LUNAR PHASES, pg. 81
1. waning gibbous moon
2. full moon
3. waxing crescent moon

LUNAR ECLIPSES, pg. 82
1. Penumbral lunar eclipse
2. Total lunar eclipse
3. Partial lunar eclipse

MORE ECLIPSES, pg. 83
1. Earth's, Moon
2. Moon's, Earth
3. corona
4. penumbra
5. 252,000
6. tilted
7. totality
8. umbra

CHAPTER 14 REVIEW, pgs. 84-85
1. To orbit means to travel around a star or planet because of the gravitational pull of the star or planet.
2. The Earth's seasons have remained the same because the gravitational pull of the Moon stabilizes the tilt of the Earth's axis.
3. The phases of the Moon are the different ways we see the Moon throughout the month.
4. The penumbra is the large, outer region of a shadow in which the Sun's light is partially blocked.
5. The umbra is the central, darker region of a shadow in which the Sun's light is totally blocked.
6. A total lunar eclipse occurs when the Moon passes through the Earth's umbra.
7. The three kinds of lunar eclipses are total lunar eclipses, penumbral lunar eclipses, and partial lunar eclipses.
8. The three kinds of solar eclipses are total solar eclipses, partial solar eclipses, and annular solar eclipses.
9. b, d
10. strongest, weakest
11. When gravity pulls on something that is very large, the object tends to become stretched.
12. penumbra
13. umbra
14. penumbra
15. umbra

Chapter 15

WHAT IS TRUE?, pg. 86
1. True
2. False
3. False
4. True
5. False
6. True
7. True
8. True
9. False
10. True
11. False
12. False

FILL IN THE BLANKS, pg. 87
1. mass
2. 865,000; 333,000
3. hydrogen
4. 11,000; 27,000,000
5. matter, matter
6. gravity
7. weight
8. reflecting
9. nuclear fusion

NUCLEAR FUSION, pg. 88
1. True
2. False
3. True
4. False
5. True
6. False
7. True
8. False
9. True
10. False
11. True

GAMMA RAYS TO SUNSHINE, pg. 89
1. False
2. True
3. True
4. False
5. True
6. False
7. True
8. True
9. False
10. False
11. True

LOW-MASS STARS, pgs. 90-91
1. white dwarf, planetary nebula
2. nuclear fusion
3. fuel
4. decreases
5. gamma rays
6. gravity
7. carbon
8. temperatures
9. mass
10. low-mass
11. planetary nebula
12. carbon
13. elephants
14. denser
15. black
16. heat

HIGH-MASS STARS AND SUPERNOVAE, pgs. 92-93
1. True
2. True
3. False
4. False
5. True
6. High-mass stars
7. High-mass stars
8. Low-mass stars
9. all stars
10. Low-mass stars
11. high-mass stars
12. all stars
13. High-mass stars
14. All stars

CHAPTER 15 REVIEW, pgs. 94-95
1. An aurora is a display of lights caused by the interaction of the solar wind with the Earth's magnetic field.
2. The solar wind is a stream of energetic particles that escape the pull of the Sun's gravity and shoot into outer space.
3. Nuclear fusion is a process in which two or more nuclei are forced to fuse, or combine, into a single, larger nucleus.
4. Gamma rays are the most energetic, powerful form of electromagnetic radiation.
5. A planetary nebula is the outer layers of a dead low-mass star.
6. A white dwarf star is the glowing ball of hot, dense carbon that remains when a low-mass star releases its outer layers in a planetary nebula.
7. A supernova is the tremendous explosion that occurs at the death of a high-mass star.
8. Carbon
9. White dwarf star
10. Iron
11. Supernova

Chapter 16

TERRESTRIAL OR JOVIAN?, pg. 96
1. False
2. True
3. False
4. True
5. False
6. True
7. True
8. True
9. True
10. False
11. True
12. True

GREENHOUSE EFFECT, pgs. 97-98
1. gravity
2. rotates
3. magnet
4. outer space
5. atmosphere
6. greenhouses
7. radiates
8. water vapor
9. infrared

FILL IN THE BLANK, pg. 98
atmosphere

JUPITER AND THE ASTEROID BELT, pgs. 99-100
1. four
2. asteroid belt
3. orbit
4. massive
5. Ceres
6. thousands
7. Jupiter
8. Sun
9. solar system
10. rotates
11. moons
12. Ganymede
13. rock, metal, ice
14. Europa
15. gravity

PLANET FACTS, pgs. 101-102
1. Mercury
2. Saturn
3. Earth
4. Venus
5. Venus
6. Jupiter
7. Jupiter
8. Neptune
9. Saturn
10. Neptune
11. Earth
12. Neptune
13. Mars
14. Mars
15. Uranus
16. Venus
17. Jupiter
18. Mercury

CHAPTER 16 REVIEW, pgs. 103-105
1. Mercury, Venus, Mars, Jupiter, Saturn
2. The terrestrial planets are made of rocks and metals, and are much closer to the Sun than the jovian planets are.
3. The jovian planets are composed mainly of hydrogen and helium gases and are much larger than the terrestrial planets.
4. The greenhouse effect is the result of greenhouse gases, which allow sunlight to pass through the atmosphere, but do not allow infrared radiation to pass back out.
5. Atmospheric pressure is the way we measure the weight of the air above our heads and the "push" of the air against our bodies.
6. You would weigh more on Jupiter than on Earth because Jupiter's enormous mass gives it an extremely strong gravitational pull.
7. The Kuiper Belt is a ring of comets and dwarf planets on the outskirts of the solar system.

8. Comets are huge chunks of ice mixed with rocks and dust.
9. Comets grow tails when they approach the Sun.
10. Meteors are rocky particles that fall through the Earth's atmosphere as shooting stars.
11. False
12. False
13. True
14. True
15. False
16. True
17. False
18. True
19. True
20. False
21. True

Chapter 17

GALAXIES AND MORE, pg. 106
1. False
2. False
3. True
4. True
5. False
6. False
7. True
8. False
9. True
10. False
11. True
12. False

BIRTH OF STARS, pg. 107
1. supernova
2. molecular, star
3. dust
4. shock waves
5. stronger
6. million
7. massive
8. hot
9. nuclear fusion
10. globule
11. rotating

WHAT IS TRUE?, pg. 108
1. False
2. False
3. False
4. True
5. True
6. False
7. True
8. True
9. True
10. True
11. False
12. False
13. False
14. True
15. True

THE BIG BANG THEORY, pgs. 109-111
1. Creation
2. space, time
3. theory
4. particles
5. atoms
6. cooler
7. billion
8. hydrogen, helium
9. 13.75
10. age
11. galactic clusters
12. stars
13. Edwin Hubble
14. Georges Lemaitre
15. Big Bang
16. creating
17. does not
18. size
19. massive
20. expand
21. short-lived, unstable
22. supernovae

CHAPTER 17 REVIEW, pgs. 112-113
1. A galaxy is a group of billions of stars.
2. There are 150 billion stars in the Milky Way.
3. Spiral galaxies are galaxies that have a central bulge surrounded by a thin disk with long, spiral arms.
4. Molecular clouds are the clouds of dust and gas in which new stars are born.
5. Globules are the thick clumps of gas and dust that turn into new stars.
6. The Big Bang theory says that the universe, including space and time, began as a huge explosion.
7. A singularity is a place that is so dense and small that scientists have no idea what goes on there.
8. The Big Bang explosion had to be exact to about 50 decimal places.
9. If the universe were less massive at the time of the Big Bang, the Big Bang would have blown all the protons and atoms apart so quickly that there would be no time for galaxies, stars, and planets to form.

Unit 3 Test

pgs. 114-115
1. b
2. a
3. b
4. b
5. b
6. b
7. c
8. c
9. a
10. c
11. a
12. b
13. c